CELTIC

CROSS STITCH
SAMPLERS

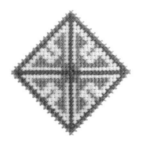

CELTIC

CROSS STITCH SAMPLERS

Angela Wainwright

CASSELL

Cassell
Wellington House
125 Strand
London WC2R 0BB

Produced by Rosemary Wilkinson
4 Lonsdale Square
London N1 1EN

First published 1995
First paperback edition 1996

Distributed in the United States
by Sterling Publishing Co., Inc.
387 Park Avenue South, New York, New York 10016-8810

Distributed in Australia
By Capricorn Link (Australia) Pty Ltd
2/13 Carrington Road
Castle Hill
NSW 2154

Design and chart artwork: Pentrix Design
Photography: Mark Gatehouse
Illustrations: Stephen Dew
Picture research: Jane Lewis
Colour reproduction: Blackjacks

British Library Cataloguing-in-Publication Data
A catalogue record for this book is available from
the British Library

ISBN 0-304-34443-5 (hardback)
ISBN 0-304-34582-2 (paperback)

Printed and bound in Hong Kong

Contents

Historical Background

The word 'Celt' is often used in a rather romantic fashion to refer collectively to those Britons, Welsh, Scots and Irish, who still speak forms of a Celtic language. Classically, though, the term has been employed since the sixth century BC to describe a group of people or tribal units who followed a particular lifestyle rather than who spoke a common language, although there have been suggestions that a form of Celtish language was spoken as far back as a thousand years before Christ. These tribal units were much more widespread than is generally supposed, with settlements across Europe into Asia Minor and south into Rome and Greece.

Their economy was based on crop growing and animal husbandry,

◆ Two enamelled pieces of horse harness from the mid-first century AD. Red was the most popular colour for enamelling and the curved design is typical of the period.

boosted at certain times of their history by trade, particularly with Mediterranean areas.

Early forms of Celtic culture can be traced as far back as the seventh century BC, through excavations at Hallstatt, a site in Austria, but a more clearly defined Celtic society, known as La Tène, is generally seen as beginning around 500 - 450 BC with a concentration of people around the Middle Rhine and Northern France. The Celtic tribal units then extended into Austria, southern France and around the Danube, and later still into the Balkans, Asia Minor, Western France and the British Isles. With distinctive cultures already well-established in these areas, the incoming Celts absorbed and incorporated the existing traditions, including those influencing design, into their own. This possibly explains some of the classical influences apparent in some Celtic work and the orientalisation in others.

In England during the period from the middle of the first century to the fifth AD, most of the country was under Roman occupation. The occupation did not extend as far as Scotland, Ireland and Wales, also

parts of Cornwall were left alone, and in these parts Celtic art forms and design continued, which may partly explain the continuing practice of skills in these areas today. For the remaining Celtic tribal units, though, Roman classical influence was strong and there is evidence, in such places as Bath, of the Celtic craftsmen having been co-opted by the Romans to help decorate their newly-built houses and public buildings. The Celts obviously used the Romans as a source of income, crafting pieces specially to sell to them and would presumably have allowed some Roman influence to modify their designs in order to make them more appealing to the buyers.

Our main sources of information about the Celts, apart from some fragmented classical writings and the recording in the seventh century AD of principally Irish and Welsh folktales, are the archaeological finds which have been excavated over the centuries. They give us a unique glimpse of the Celtic way of life, rich and poor alike, and it is from the large collection of artefacts that inspiration for design work emulating Celtic styles in succeeding centuries has derived. These finds do not, however, provide the complete picture, which has only led to a greater fascination with and a stronger desire to know more about this ancient, highly creative culture; indeed, the revival of interest in the culture can be traced as far back as the Renaissance. Europe was positively obsessed with all things Celtic.

◆ The triskele is one of the most common motifs in Celtic art, to be found on both metalwork and illuminated manuscripts.

A great many of the artefacts discovered are of metalwork, understandable, of course, because of its higher durability as against wood or stone, so that we have many examples of jewellery, domestic implements, horse harness paraphernalia and battle-dress. The pieces are evidence of the high level of the decorative skills of the Celtic craftsmen, who were most probably supported by an apprenticeship scheme and would have worked on a commission basis, in the first place travelling to work on site and later having a place in fully established workshops.

There is little doubt that much of this metalwork was made for trading in exchange for wine, etc., in order to sustain the lifestyles of the chiefs. The wooden and stone artefacts seem to have been more directly of personal or religious significance.

The Celtic culture was always receptive to change and its artistic development was essentially fluid. As already mentioned, it was constantly absorbing and responding to new learning, whether from classical sources or from exploring its own style. It is important to note, though, that despite the Celts' ready acceptance of outside influences, these never dominated.

Celtic art is generally abstract and non-narrative, tales being left to the storytellers and the scribes. The Celts gave due deference to their gods, but do not seem to have represented them heavily in their decorative artwork: plant forms are much more common, which is understandable in a culture where the lifestyle was essentially agricultural. However, a study of the abstract designs shows that various motifs and emblems, such as the triskeles (see opposite) and particular animals and birds, were featured repeatedly, which leads us to believe that they must have had a symbolic significance. The motifs on personal possessions, for instance, are often executed in such a delicate way that they must have had great importance either to the owner or the embellisher and the richly-ornamented stone slabs of the Pictish carvers in northern

◆ A well-preserved example of Pictish stone carving from a churchyard in Aberlemno, Scotland.

Scotland (known as the Cruithre) contain knotwork, key and spiral designs which are not found anywhere else, so must have been of particular significance to these people.

The main features of Celtic design work, then, are the knotwork and key patterns, as well as flowing plant, animal and human forms. It is a fascinating mix of mathematical exactness and free-form shapes. The Celtic artists showed a marvellous grasp of abstract pattern in their undulating lines and spiral patterns which often played around or turned into recognisable shapes.

Knotwork consists of an over-and-under interlaced ribbon design, whereas the key patterns are made up of interlocking geometric shapes. Plant forms include lotus buds and palmettes (petal decorations radiating like palm fronds), while living creatures are represented by often-stylised depictions of boars, horses, birds and human masks. Abstract motifs include lyre-shaped scrolls and triskeles - three-legged wheels. The triskele is one of the most predominant and important of Celtic motifs. Three was a magic number for the Celts, so it was a powerful symbol in their designs.

The period of the Celtic culture covers different phases. Paul Jacobsthal, an eminent archaeologist of the 1930s, established three distinct styles of Celtic art. The first, called 'early style' is represented by pieces from the Hallstatt site and designs derived from Greek art. This phase begins around 8 BC, when the working of iron first became apparent in Europe, and extends to the close of the sixth century BC. Halstatt designs were extremely simple; even at their most complex they were no more than series of circles linked with lines. Cross-hatched triangles, arcs and dots were decorated onto bronze and iron scabbards and dagger sheaths, while the Greek influence produced designs with more fluid lines, including palmettes and lotus buds, which decorated domestic appliances and implements of war.

The second style Jacobsthal designated 'Waldalgesheim' style, named after artefacts found in a princess' grave at Wald. It is also known as 'vegetal style'. This, as its alternative name implies, concentrated more on plant forms (influenced by Italy) with the lotus buds and palmettes now worked with many flowing tendrils in continuous designs, into which faces were intertwined, giving a feeling of movement and fluidity.

The third style, 'plastic style' or 'sword style', covers the designs of the later third and second centuries BC, so-called since most of the excavated pieces are iron swords and scabbards, featuring a more asymmetrical approach to the vegetal style, together with lyre shapes, often incorporating dragons' heads and other creatures. As the style developed, the creatures gained tails to add to the complexity of shape. Flower motifs still continued to be used but in more complicated designs, interlaced with spirals, and zoomorphic heads growing out of interwoven tendrils.

In the second and first centuries AD there was less innovation in

Celtic design and an increase of classical influence (in particular, Roman, as mentioned previously) together with a more naturalistic style. Animal and human figures were still present but plant forms became rarer. The decorative design on swords, for example, became more anthropomorphic. In Ireland, traditions continued unabated for many centuries and reflowered in mainland Britain after the departure of the Romans in AD 140. The major source of influence on Celtic art after this departure was the flowering of Christianity, the fusion of the two cultures creating such beautiful manuscripts as the Book of Durrow, the Book of Kells and the Lindisfarne Gospels, the latter two of which I have drawn upon extensively for design inspiration. The majority of other design sources I have used for this volume are taken from pre-Roman Celtic art forms.

And so to work!

◆ A detail showing the wonderfully intricate illumination in the Lindisfarne Gospels.

15

Psalter Sampler

In keeping with the original 'exemplaire' of generations of past needle-women, I felt it important to include a piece of work with the same concept in mind, that is, a piece of work which will display a wide range of different patterns as evidence of the skill of the embroiderer. One of the aims of this book is to inspire the reader to look beyond my designs and make his or her own detailed study of the period and its decorative art forms. This project is really, then, a 'pattern book', serving as an introduction to some of the main elements of Celtic design. Here are some fine examples of key patterns, scrolls and knotwork taken from the Book of Kells, the Lindisfarne Gospels, the Colliburn Stone and a bronze belt plaque. Many of these sources are shown on the following pages. The scrolled shape in the centre is taken from the Vespasian psalter, shown on page 32.

The sampler can be worked as a complete project in its own right, it can be personalised as a commemorative sampler by omitting the central psalter design and replacing it with relevant names, dates, etc., or the various designs contained within each section can be extracted and used as the basis for other projects. The three projects on pages 24 to 27 show some of the possibilities.

I have taken a little designer's licence, so that instead of laying the different patterns in bands, as would have been the case in the old samplers, I have used the shape of an ornamental text page in the Book of Kells to give form to the project.

◆ Left: The page from the Book of Kells which is the inspiration for the shape of this sampler.
Right: The Psalter Sampler in style and shape is representative of and inspired by the marvellous Celtic illuminated manuscripts.

MATERIALS

*1 piece of cream Aida, 16 count, 16 x 20 in
(40 x 51 cm)*

tapestry needle, size 26

lightweight wadding for mounting (optional)

*1 skein each of stranded cotton in the
following shades:*

		DMC	Anchor
	dusky pink	315	896
	turquoise	597	168
	brown	632	936
	grey	413	401
	purple	327	100
	pale pink	3354	74
	acid green	472	278
	burnished gold	832	907
	light burnished gold	834	874
	leaf green	471	265
	lilac	553	98
	mauve	209	109
	deep pink	3685	69
	dull mauve	3041	871
	dark pink	3687	68
	medium pink	3688	66
	dark blue	825	162
	blue green	502	877
	red	816	44
	jade	991	189
	dull blue	930	922
	light brown	3772	914
	light blue green	564	206
	dark red	902	72
	light blue	800	144
	white	blanc	1

*3 skeins each of stranded cotton in the
following shades:*

	yellow	726	295
	blue	793	176

Finished size: 10¼ x 13¼ in (26 x 33.5 cm)

◆ **Right: King Solomon's Knot:
a popular knotwork design.
Far right: A detail from the
Lindisfarne Gospels, adapted for the
circle design on the Psalter Sampler.**

METHOD

As this is quite a detailed project that will take some time to complete, I strongly recommend that you hem or tack the raw edges of the fabric before starting to cross stitch, to prevent fraying (see page 90).

Fold the fabric in half lengthwise to find the centre vertical line and crease lightly. Now measure down this fold for 3 in (7.5 cm) from the top of the fabric. This will give the point at which you start stitching on the fabric. Find the starting stitch marked on the chart on page 21 and begin work on the fabric with this stitch.

Use two strands of cotton, working over one thread intersection. Work the outlines in back stitch and the rest in cross stitch.

Stitch this sampler in blocks, i.e. complete each different pattern and its surrounding border before moving on to the next, working either horizontally or vertically from the starting point. In a complex pattern grouping such as this design, it is essential that the allocated number of stitches is adhered to, otherwise the blocks will not fit together, so do keep checking the positioning of the stitched blocks against each other and the chart.

When the stitching is completed, wash if necessary and press gently from the wrong side (see page 90). For finishing and mounting instructions, see page 92.

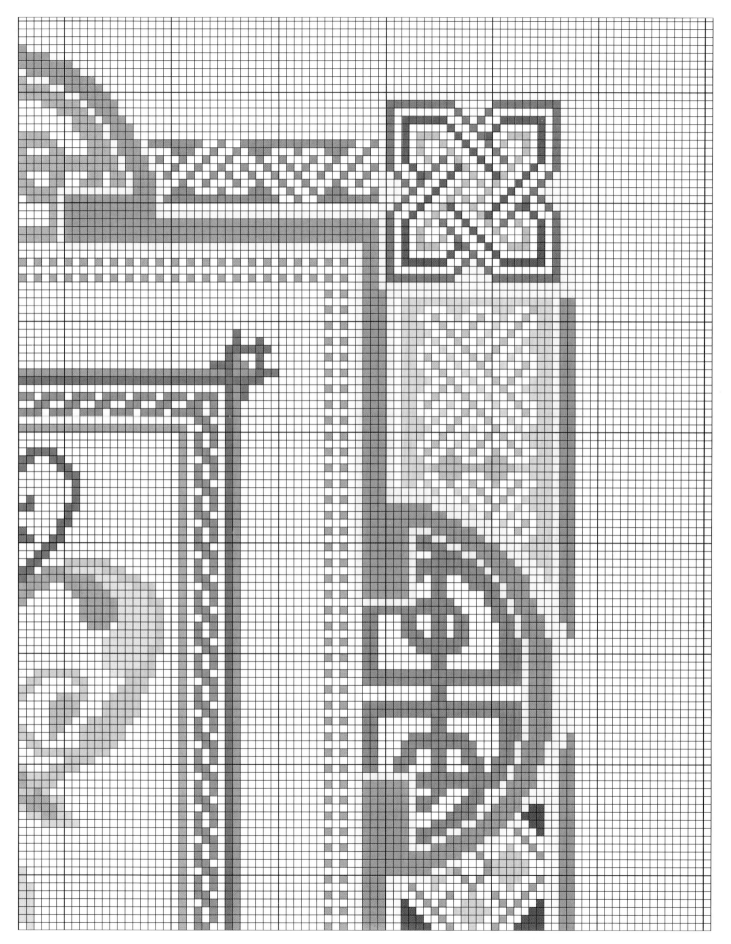

MATERIALS

(Napkins)

1 set of white Sal-Em napkins, 26 count
(see page 93 for stockists)

tapestry needle, size 24

1 skein each of stranded cotton in the
following shades:

		DMC	Anchor
	green	471	265
	light brown	950	4146
	gold green	472	278
	brown	3773	882

Finished size of design (single square):
2 x 2 in (5 x 5 cm)

MATERIALS

(Traycloth)

1 piece of cream linen, 28 count,
17 x 14¾ in (43 x 37.5 cm)

tapestry needle, size 24 or 26

1 skein each of stranded cotton in the
following shades:

		DMC	Anchor
	dark blue	798	131
	powder blue	809	130
	light blue	800	144
	green	954	203
	yellow	743	305

Finished size of design: 8¼ x 1⅓ in
(21 x 3.5 cm)

◆ **Far right: Drawing on sources used
for the Psalter Sampler, these two
pieces of table linen show alternative
applications for the motifs.**

Napkins

This is the first of several projects showing how sections of the large samplers can be isolated and used on smaller pieces. This simple knotwork design, commonly used in early manuscripts, was called in later times 'King Solomon's Knot' (see page 18), as it was supposed that all the wisdom of Solomon was hidden in the knot. To the early Christian monks, the square's geometry may have symbolised the three-in-one or trinity of Father, Son and Holy Ghost.

A set of napkins with this design will perhaps stimulate wise after-dinner conversation! The design is worked in a group of three squares to continue the symbolism. It can be worked in just one or in all four corners.

METHOD

Count eight threads up from the fray-stop line of stitching at the bottom of the napkin and eight threads in from the stitching line at the side. Begin work at this point following the starting stitch marked on the chart below.

Work in cross stitch using three strands of cotton over two threads of the fabric. When the stitching is complete, press the fabric gently from the wrong side.

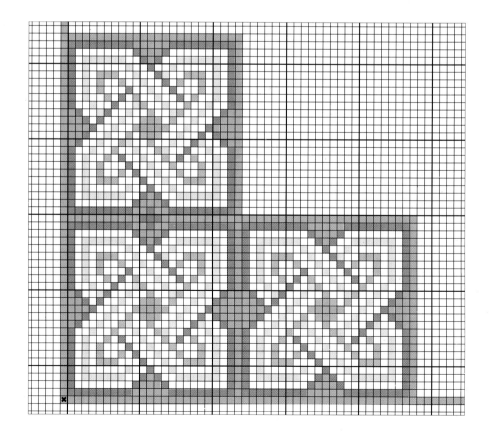

Traycloth

The source material itself, as well as the designs I have adapted from them, provide scope for further exploration. Here is another, seemingly more complex, design motif from the Book of Kells which is, in fact, based on a simple diamond shape. In the original it has been drawn as a decoration on the two creatures on either side of the figure of St Matthew (see page 26).

Here it is used as a border for a traycloth but you could experiment with the pattern repeat to shape it into a square block and use it on a cushion front. It could also be used as it stands to embroider a Christmas cake band, in which case, choose reds, greens and golds for the threads.

METHOD

Machine a line of stay stitching round all four sides of the linen ⅜ in (1 cm) in from the edge, then fray the edges beyond this line. The design is worked on the short side of the cloth. With the short sides at top and bottom, fold the fabric in half lengthwise. Count eight threads up this centre line from the fray-stop line of stitching and begin work at this point following the stitch marked on the chart on the right.

Work in cross stitch using two strands of cotton over two threads of the fabric.

When the stitching is complete, press the fabric gently from the wrong side.

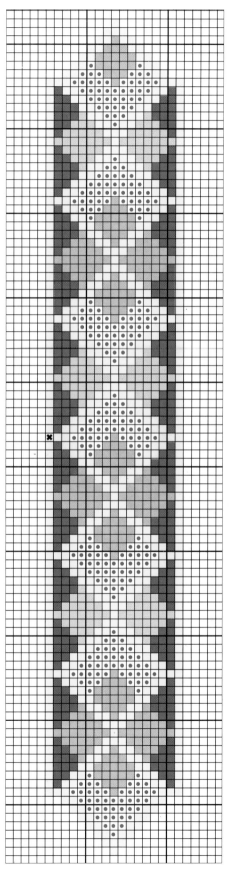

Wooden Pot

A small design taken from the Book of Kells, St Matthew's Gospel, another part of which was used in the Psalter Sampler on page 17. This is a useful little motif to have in your collection for corners of frames or the centre of a napkin perhaps. The card on page 59 is worked in the same shades, so that you can use leftover threads from one project on the other.

METHOD

Fold the fabric in half lengthwise and crosswise to find the centre point. Crease lightly. Start at this point following the stitch marked on the chart opposite. Work the cross stitch using two strands of cotton over one thread intersection. Work the back stitch using one strand of cotton over one thread intersection.

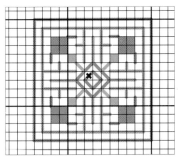

When the stitching is complete, press the fabric gently from the wrong side. Place the interfacing centrally on the reverse of the work and iron in position. Trim and mount the piece for the pot lid following the manufacturer's instructions.

MATERIALS

1 piece of white Aida, 18 count, 4 x 4 in (10 x 10 cm)

1 piece of iron-on interfacing, same size as the Aida

tapestry needle, size 26

1 wooden pot, diameter 3 in (7.5 cm)

1 skein each of stranded cotton in the following shades:

		DMC	Anchor
	green	733	280
	brown	680	901

Finished size of design: 1 1/8 x 1 1/8 in (2.8 x 2.8 cm)

◆ Far left: The Book of Kells is a rich source of design inspiration. This is the opening page of the Gospel of St Matthew from which I have taken three motifs: the cross-cornering for the Psalter Sampler on page 17; the diamond decoration on the creatures for the traycloth (page 25) and the latticework on the robe for the little wooden pot shown on this page.

MATERIALS

1 piece of white Aida, 14 count, 5 x 5 in (12 x 12 cm)

1 piece of iron-on interfacing, same size as the Aida

tapestry needle, size 24

1 desk pen set (see page 93 for stockists)

1 skein each of stranded cotton in the following shades:

		DMC	Anchor
▮	purple	327	100
▮	green	3346	267
▮	bronze	832	907

Finished size of design: 2¼ x 2¼ in (5.5 x 5.5 cm)

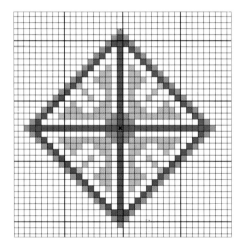

Desk Pen Set

Looking more closely at the canon page opposite, it's possible to extract small circular motifs from the tops of the columns between the gospel cross references. Any one of these could be used; I have taken the small key pattern from the second column from the left and worked it singly to make a design for a desk pen set. It could be used in a variety of other ways by repeating the design in blocks to make an enlarged diamond or in rows for a border pattern.

METHOD

Fold the fabric in half lengthwise and crosswise to find the centre point. Crease lightly. Begin work at this point following the starting stitch marked on the chart on the left.

Work in cross stitch using three strands of cotton over one thread intersection.

When the stitching is complete, press the fabric gently from the wrong side. Place the interfacing centrally on the reverse of the work and iron in position. Trim and place the fabric centrally in the mount following the manufacturer's instructions.

◆ From the same design source as the previous project, this key pattern is appropriately displayed in a penholder.

Book Cover

A corner triangular infill decoration taken from the same canon page of the Book of Kells as the half moons on the Psalter Sampler forms the four corners of this design, leaving a central diamond in which you can work one of the other designs featured in the book. Alternatively, you might wish to personalise the piece with a name in the centre and perhaps a small design.

This project has been designed as a book cover but it could also be used as a clock decoration, using one of the specially manufactured clock cases (see page 93) or, on a larger count of fabric, as a cushion front. Alternatively, a block calendar could be attached to the centre and doweling rods threaded through at top and bottom, as for the Alphabet Sampler on page 37, to create a wall hanging.

METHOD

Measure 3 in (7.5 cm) down from the top right corner of the fabric and 3 in (7.5 cm) in from the righthand side, and begin stitching at this point following the point marked on the chart on page 30.

Work the cross stitch using two strands of cotton over one thread intersection. Work the back stitch on the grid design using one strand of cotton over one thread intersection and on the internal diamond using two strands of cotton over one thread intersection.

When the stitching is completed, press lightly from the wrong side, then turn under a ½ in (12 mm) hem all round and stitch down. Place the interfacing centrally on the reverse of the work, trim it so that it is just a little shorter all round, then iron in place.

This panel can now be attached to a book cover you can make from contrasting fabric. Wrap the paper around the book you wish to cover and make a pattern, including book flaps. Add ½ in (12 mm) hem allowance to all edges. Cut out the fabric to this pattern. Turn under the ½ in (12 mm) hem and stitch down. Place in position round the book and pin the cross-stitched panel to the front of the cover in the desired position. Slip stitch neatly in place and, if you so wish, add braid round the edges. Finally slip stitch the cover flaps to form pockets to take the book covers.

◆ **A canon page from the Book of Kells.**

MATERIALS

1 piece of white Aida, 18 count, 10 x 10 in (26.5 x 26.5 cm)

1 piece of iron-on interfacing, same size as the Aida

tapestry needle, size 26

fabric for book cover, e.g. heavy cotton, velvet (see method)

large piece of scrap paper

1 yard (1 metre) braid (optional)

1 skein each of stranded cotton in the following shades:

		DMC	Anchor
	blue	813	160
	brown	832	907
	yellow	727	293

plus the shades needed for your choice of central motif or lettering.

Finished size of design: 4 1/8 x 4 1/8 in (10.5 x 10.5 cm)

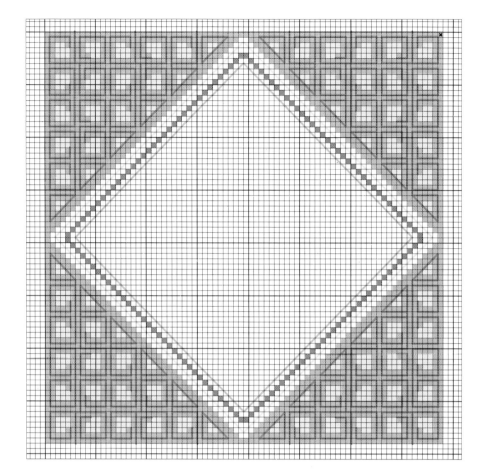

◆ From the inside to the outside of a book: a design inspired by one of the canon pages in the Book of Kells.

Evening Bag

The motif for this evening bag is the central shape of the Psalter Sampler on page 17, which was inspired by an English psalter of the second quarter of the 8th century. The plate is entitled 'David and his Musicians'. Using some metallic threads and working on a black ground gives a quite different look to the design, but you could copy the colours from the sampler and work on a lighter fabric if preferred. If you have already worked the sampler, you will have plenty of leftover threads to reproduce the motif on the bag.

Used here to decorate an evening bag, the motif could also be worked as a book cover or for a similar project where a full single motif is required and could be framed by one of the other border designs shown on the sampler.

METHOD

Fold the fabric in half, lengthwise, to find the centre vertical line. Crease lightly. Measure 2 1/2 in (6 cm) up this centre line from the bottom of the fabric. This places the centre starting stitch on the fabric, as marked on the chart on page 32. Position the design so that the base faces the lower edge.

Using two strands of cotton over one thread intersection, work the complete motif in cross stitch.

When completed, press the work gently on the wrong side. If using interfacing, work as follows. Position the interfacing over the wrong side of the Aida and iron in place. Place the lining on the right side of the Aida and pin. Machine stitch or back stitch around three sides, one of which is the motif end, leaving a 3/8 in (1 cm) seam allowance.

If using wadding, the sequence is as follows. Place the Aida fabric right side up. Position the lining on top, then the wadding on top of the lining. Pin and machine or hand stitch as above.

Turn right side out, turn under the seam allowance on the open side and slip stitch to close. Fold the piece into three with the lining on the inside, so that the embroidered section forms a flap over the top which hangs just short of the fold (leaving room for a button, if using). Oversew the two short sides of the unworked section to form a pouch.

A tassel can be attached centrally on the decorated flap to finish. Alternatively for a more secure finish, sew a button onto the pouch section and work a loop in the corresponding position on the flap.

◆ The decorative device on this evening bag has been lifted straight from an old English psalter. It works equally well against a black background as here or a pale one as in the Psalter Sampler on page 17.

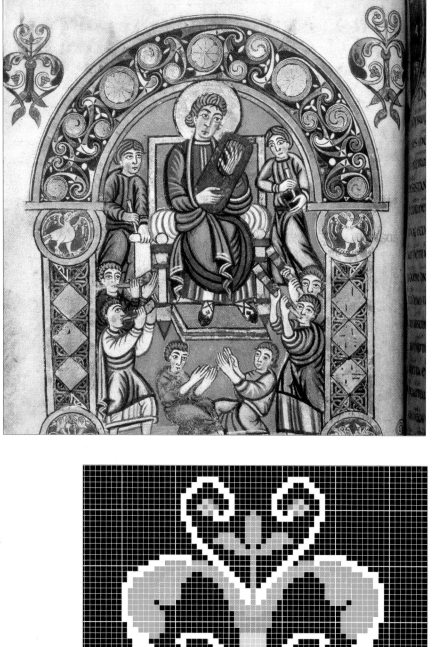

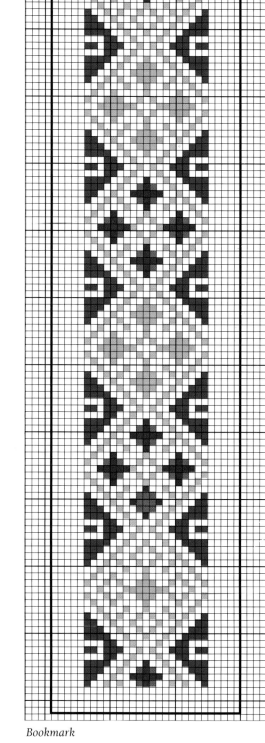

Evening bag

Bookmark

Kells Bookmark

This bookmark takes one of the more complex designs from the Psalter Sampler, where it is shown in a wider repeated form and adapts it to fit the long, narrow shape of a bookmark. The design was inspired by a folio from the Book of Kells described on page 35. The same shades of stranded cotton have been used as in the original design, so if you have worked the sampler, you should be able to use the leftover threads for this bookmark.

METHOD

Fold the bookmark in half lengthwise to find the centre vertical line and mark this at the top with a pin. Check

the number of threads per inch on the bookmark against the chart on page 32. The bookmark counts can vary by one or two squares; if there is a discrepancy, adjust the design accordingly, so that it is centred on the bookmark. Count down the same number of threads on the fabric as there are squares on the design chart (allowing for any discrepancy) and begin work with the starting stitch given on the chart.

Work in cross stitch using two strands of cotton over one thread intersection.

When the stitching is completed, wash if necessary and press gently from the wrong side (see page 90).

MATERIALS

(Bookmark)

1 lacy bookmark (see page 93 for stockists)

tapestry needle, size 26

1 skein each of stranded cotton in the following shades:

		DMC	Anchor
■	dull blue	930	922
■	dark red	902	72
	light burnished		
▨	gold	834	874
▨	blue green	502	877

Finished size of design: 1⅛ x 6¼ in (3 x 16 cm)

MATERIALS

(Evening bag)

2 pieces of black Aida, 18 count, 10 x 24¼ in (25 x 61.5 cm)

1 piece of lining material, same size as the Aida

tapestry needle, size 24 or 26

heavyweight interfacing or lightweight wadding, same size as the Aida

1 tassel or button as clasp

black sewing thread and sharp-pointed needle

1 skein each of stranded cotton in the following shades:

		DMC	Anchor
▨	pink	604	55
▨	green	563	208
□	white	blanc	1
▨	gold metallic		
▨	silver metallic		

Finished size (single unit of design): 2¾ x 3½ in (7 x 9 cm)

◆ **Left:** This decorative page comes from the Vespasian psalter dating from the 8th century AD.
Above: The bookmark is a good shape for trying out some of the border designs in the Celtic manuscripts.

Alphabet Sampler

There is little doubt that the tradition of manuscript writing in the British Isles originates with the Irish, who in turn developed the art from transcription brought to Ireland from Italy.

The oldest book, The Book of Durrow, shows a definite mingling of Mediterranean, Germanic and Celtic styles. For this volume, however, I have decided to concentrate on the Lindisfarne Gospels and the Book of Kells as manuscript design sources, as I feel their beauty is particularly fine.

Celtic influence was still strong during the 7th and 8th centuries AD when these were compiled. The Lindisfarne Gospels, compiled at the place of its title, has a well-documented history: the colophon at the end of the book, attached by Alfred who translated it from the Latin into Anglo-Saxon English some 250 years after its construction, tells us that the book was written by Eadfrith, Bishop of Lindisfarne, was bound by Ethelward and the cover embellished by Billfrith. The Gospels were written in reverence to God and St Cuthbert and it has been estimated that Eadfrith must have worked continuously for at least two years.

In two texts now, though originally only in Latin, the book is divided into the Four Gospels, and intended as an altar book, perhaps being used only then on special occasions. The text is written in almost black ink containing carbon or soot black, and quill or reed pens were used to execute the lettering.

The decoration of the pages seems to have been first worked out mathematically with a series of prick marks, rules and compass holes laid down on the vellum. These then serve as a pattern over which the decoration was drawn by eye, having probably been practised on a wax tablet - the

◆ **Far left: A text page from St Matthew in the Book of Kells showing the many facets of Celtic design.**
Below: A marvellously complex page from the Lindisfarne Gospels: this is the carpet page for St Luke's Gospel.

MATERIALS

1 piece of beige Lugana, 25 count, 10 x 24 in (25 x 61 cm)

iron-on interfacing, 8 x 18 in (20 x 45 cm)

tapestry needle, size 24

1 pair of bell pull ends, 8 in (20 cm) in length

4 tassels (optional)

sewing cotton to match linen and sharp-pointed needle

1 skein each of stranded cotton in the following shades:

		DMC	Anchor
	light brown	436	363
	black	310	403
	blue	826	161
	red	350	11
	lilac	210	108
	dark lilac	208	111
	gold brown	831	277
	yellow	744	301
	bronze	832	907
	green	989	242
	aqua	959	186

Finished size of design: 7 x 14 in (18 x 35.5 cm)

general notebook of days gone by. A marvellous range of colours was used but special mention must be made of the blue made from lapis lazuli which was only obtainable from Afghanistan and the Himalayan foothills. How much the scribes and illustrators must have loved the brilliant blue to take so much trouble to obtain it. The binding medium for the colours was most probably egg white and fish glue.

Of direct concern as source material to this book are the decorated pages of the Gospels which fall into two categories: 'canon pages' and 'carpet pages'. 'Canon pages' contain lists of cross references to similar texts and these lists are embellished with arched and column borders, heavily decorated with fret, key and knotwork and interlaced birds. 'Carpet pages' are highly decorated introductory pages and contain a myriad examples of every conceivable Celtic pattern. Full colour miniatures of the saints and the remaining major decorated pages are also heavily ornamented: each based on either a cross or an initial followed by further letters on which every nook and cranny has been packed with patterns.

Within these pages lies the inspiration for the alphabet sampler hanging. The letters are taken both from the Lindisfarne Gospels and the Book of Kells while the birds and the knotwork are sourced just from the Gospels. The bird motifs are taken from plate 19, a carpet page introducing St Jerome's letter to Pope Damascus, shown on page 35.

A complete project in itself, the alphabet can also be used throughout the book on designs that need personalisation. It has been used on the two commemorative samplers which follow, as an illustration.

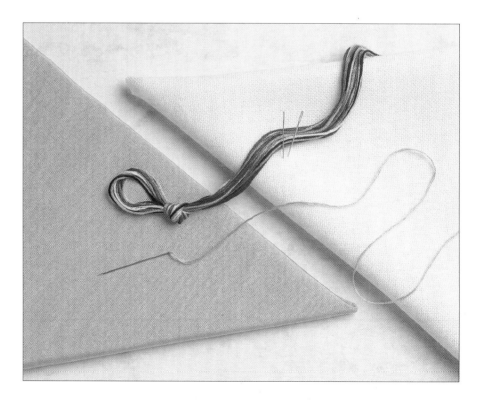

◆ **Far right: The style of the letters of this Alphabet Sampler is based on text in the Celtic illuminated manuscripts. The bird motifs are adapted from a carpet page in the Lindisfarne Gospels.**

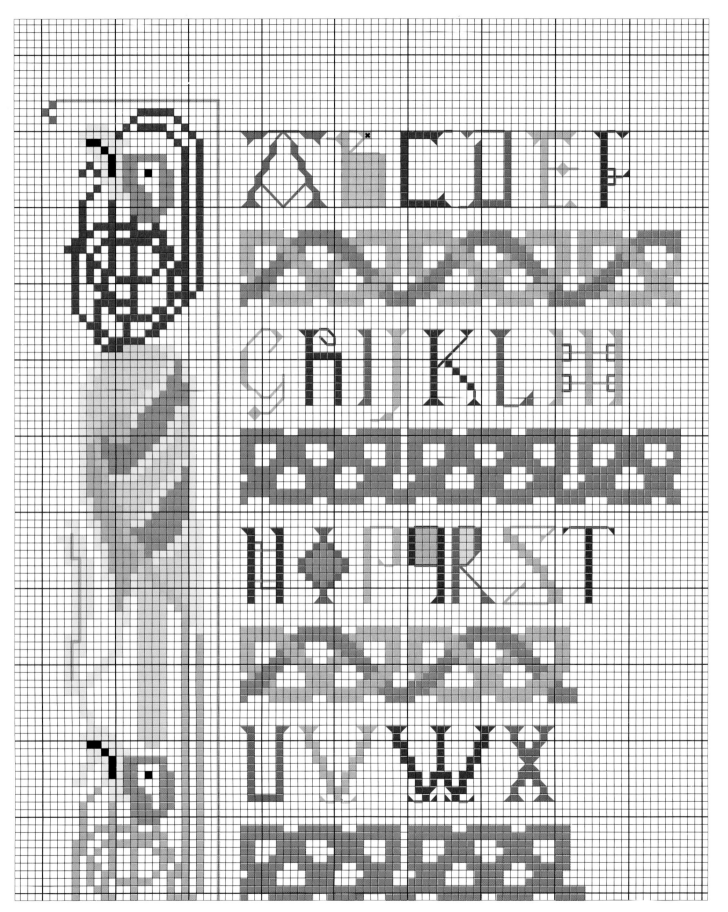

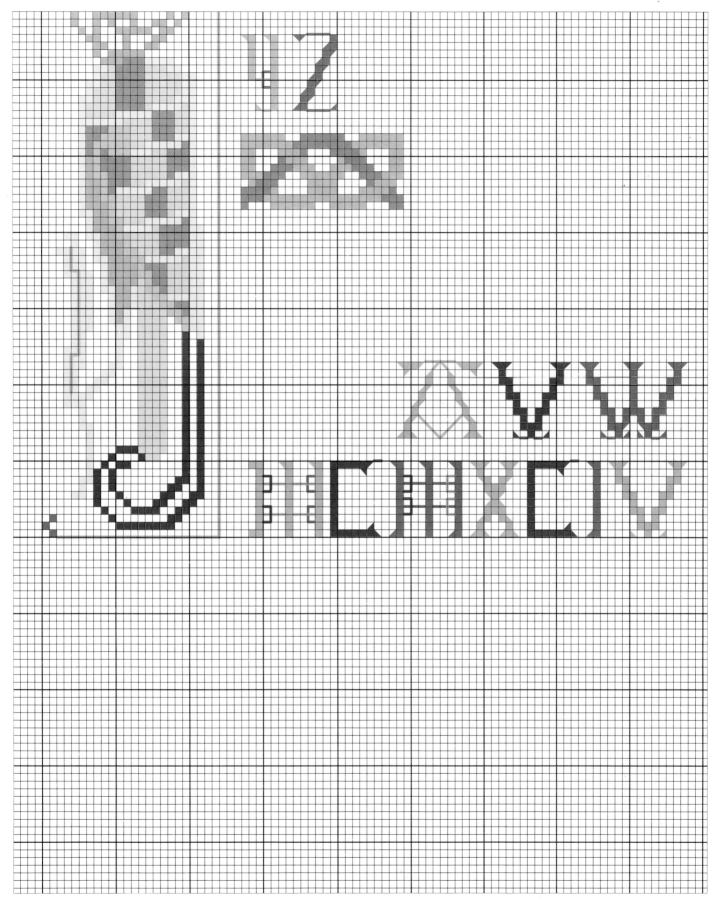

METHOD

Hem the long sides of the fabric with a ½ in (12 mm) hem. Fold the fabric in half lengthwise to find the centre vertical line. Crease lightly. Measure 5 in (12 cm) down this centre line from the top of the fabric. This places the centre starting stitch on the fabric, as marked on the chart on page 38.

Use three strands over two thread intersections. Work the narrow lines on the letters and the outlines in back stitch, the rest in cross stitch.

From the starting point work the rest of the letters in the row to the left, then concentrate on the bird motifs. Once you have completed this vertical band you will be able to double check on the positioning of subsequent horizontal lines of letters. Personalise your work by adding your name and the date of working, expressed in Roman numerals, at the base of the hanging.

When the stitching is complete, wash if necessary and press gently from the wrong side (see page 90). Place the interfacing centrally on the wrong side of the linen, so that there is a 2 in (5 cm) border of fabric left free at top and bottom, and iron in position. Fold over ¼ in (6 mm) of this border of fabric to the wrong side, then fold again, making a hem deep enough to allow the bell pull end to slot through. Slipstitch the base of this hem to secure. Repeat with the bottom hem. Insert the bell pull ends and, if using tassels, attach them to either side at the top, then hang the sampler from a picture hook.

◆ Even the text pages of the Lindisfarne Gospels are richly-ornamented as this first page of St Luke's Gospel demonstrates.

Intertwined Border and Floral Commemorative Samplers

The designs for these two commemorative samplers have been taken from the Book of Kells, another of the great manuscripts but whose origins are much more obscure than those of the Lindisfarne Gospels.

In Latin text, of the Four Gospels only two of the 680 pages are without colour. It is a large book, measuring 13 x 9½ in (33 x 24 cm), and like the Lindisfarne Gospels was designed to be kept on the altar and used for special occasions.

Its place of origin, or at least of completion, was the Kells monastery in Ireland, which became a major house after the evacuation of the Iona monastery following on attacks from Scandinavia. There are no records to tell us the identity of the scribes. The last folios are unfortunately missing and these may well have held the key to this information.

Similar in organisation to the Lindisfarne Gospels with canon tables and carpet pages (see page 36), it is considered that its text draws on more than one source. No other book of its kind has such closely

◆ **The fantastically complex interlacing on this folio from the Book of Kells is a prime example of the skill of the Celtic illuminators.**

intertwined lettering and decoration and one feels the scribes may well also have been the illustrators. As well as the large illuminated pages there are others with smaller but none the less intricate designs worked around a large initial letter. The accompanying text is heavily interlaced with designs and symbols. Animals and birds feature strongly, sometimes humorously. Snakes, mice, cats, hens and fish cavort amongst or peep out from between the complex spiral, fret and key patterns. Plants, too, have their place, forming gentle loops and twists among the text or the pattern work.

The first and larger of these two samplers is taken from a detail at the end of the Genealogy of Christ section, used here as a deep border to form the base of a commemorative sampler. I particularly loved the fluidity of line and the interweaving of the curls. It is abstract enough to be adaptable to many themes, whether a birth, a marriage or an anniversary. Use the letters from the Alphabet Sampler on pages 38 - 9 to add your own personal details.

METHOD

This, like all the samplers, is a detailed project which will take some time to complete, so I recommend that you hem or tack the raw edges of the fabric before starting to cross stitch, to prevent fraying (see page 90).

Measure 3 in (7.5 cm) up from the bottom right corner of the fabric and 3 in (7.5 cm) in from the righthand side, and begin work at this point following the starting stitch marked on the chart on page 45.

Work in cross stitch using two strands of cotton over one thread intersection.

Work the solid lower horizontal line and the two vertical lines first for approximately 100 stitches in each direction. This will give you a good reference line for the decoration. Next, work the yellow corner motif and continue working horizontally or vertically using the multi-needle approach (see page 91). Do not try to work all of one particular shade first, since one slip in counting will mean that the patterns will not connect properly. It's much better to complete each individual section, building up the design with all four colours.

To add personal details, follow the instructions on letter spacing given on page 92. When the stitching is completed, wash if necessary and press gently from the wrong side (see page 90). For finishing and mounting instructions, see page 92.

MATERIALS

1 piece of white Aida, 16 count, 20 x 20 in (51 x 51 cm)

tapestry needle, size 24

lightweight wadding for mounting (optional)

2 skeins of stranded cotton in the following shade:

		DMC	Anchor
	brown	3772	914

4 skeins of stranded cotton in:

		DMC	Anchor
	blue	809	130
	yellow	727	293
	green	563	208

plus your own choice of shade for the wording.

Finished size of design: 12 ¾ x 14 ¾ in (32.5 x 37.5 cm)

◆ **Left: These swirling, interlaced curves make an impressive border for a special occasion sampler.**

dotted lines
represent 97 stitches
containing 6 repeated
border motifs

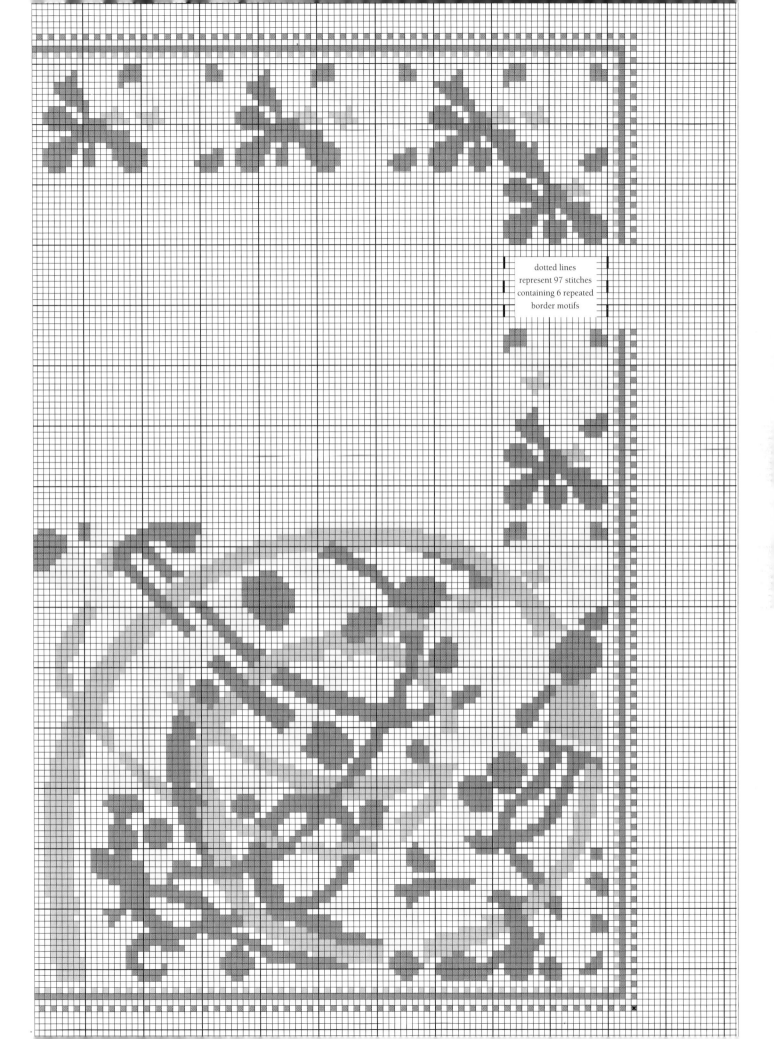

dotted lines
represent 97 stitches
containing 6 repeated
border motifs

MATERIALS

*1 piece of white Aida, 18 count, 20 x 16 in
(51 x 40 cm)*

tapestry needle, size 26

lightweight wadding for mounting (optional)

*1 skein each of stranded cotton in the
following shades:*

		DMC	Anchor
	pink	604	55
	blue	340	118
	yellow	726	295
	green	988	243

2 skeins of stranded cotton in:

	peach	353	6

*Finished size of design: 10 ⅓ x 6 ⅔ in
(26 x 17 cm)*

Floral Sampler

The source for this simpler piece is taken from the Book of Kells folio showing the Illustration of the Arrest. Undefined botanically, a colourful array of flowers weave themselves around the border. They have been adapted to decorate a rectangular frame within which you can stitch your own personal message.

METHOD

As on the previous sampler, I recommend that you hem or tack the raw edges of the fabric before starting to cross stitch, in order to prevent fraying (see page 90).

Measure 5 in (12.5 cm) down from the top right corner of the fabric and 5 in (12.5 cm) in from the righthand side, and begin work at this point following the starting stitch marked on the chart on page 48.

Work in cross stitch using two strands of cotton over one thread intersection.

Stitch the border line first, working horizontally to the upper left corner, then vertically down the lefthand side to the flower motif. Next work the vertical border on the right, followed by the lower horizontal border up to the main motif.

Note: Left-handed stitchers may wish to reverse this procedure by starting in the upper left corner.

Stitch the small corner motifs next and finally the large motif. Personalise your work by using the alphabet shown in the sampler on pages 38-9, placing the letters either next to the starting point on the chart or centrally using the method described on page 92.

When the stitching is completed, wash if necessary and press gently from the wrong side (see page 90). For finishing and mounting instructions, see page 92.

◆ Left: The little flowers and their curling stems which decorate the text over this illustration from the Book of Kells have been adapted to ornament the frame of the simple floral sampler shown on the right.

Horses Sampler

Drawing from various sources, this decorative sampler is a simple project demonstrating some fret and keywork panels typical of Celtic design. The intertwined horses are taken from the carving on the Aberlemno stone cross to be found in a churchyard in Angus, Scotland which shows the animals in the 'sword style' of later Celtic design. This cross slab is a typical Pictish monument, with a battle scene on one side and a characteristically-shaped cross on the other. The style of the spiral birds is similar to patterns in the Lindisfarne Gospels, which dates this cross at around the beginning of the eighth century AD.

The horizontal cross border and the outer key pattern border are popular Celtic patterns found on stone carvings and metalwork as well as in the illuminated manuscripts. The corner motifs show fretwork from the Lindisfarne Gospels.

METHOD

First of all I recommend that you hem or tack the raw edges of the fabric before starting to cross stitch, to prevent fraying (see page 90).

Measure 3 in (7.5 cm) down from the top right corner of the fabric and 3 in (7.5 cm) in from the righthand side and begin stitching at this point, following the starting point marked on the chart on page 51.

Use two strands of cotton for the cross stitch, working over two thread intersections. Work all lines and borders in back stitch, using two strands of black. Outline the horses in black with back stitch, using one strand of cotton.

Work in blocks, completing each one before commencing the next pattern piece and its surrounding border. This will help to prevent miscalculations of border stitches. Stitch the corner box pattern first, then continue with either the vertical or horizontal border but leave it unboxed until you have worked the relevant inner pattern.

Left-handed stitchers may wish to start in the upper left corner.

When the stitching is completed, wash if necessary and press gently from the wrong side (see page 90). For finishing and mounting instructions, see page 92.

◆ Two sources of inspiration for the Horses sampler shown on page 50: the Aberlemno cross (below) is formed from a single slab 7 feet (over 2 metres) high and is heavily carved on both sides; the interlaced ribbon pattern (above) is a design commonly found in Celtic manuscripts.

MATERIALS

1 piece of white Belfast linen, 32 count, size 16 x 14 in (40 x 35.5 cm)

tapestry needle, size 24 or 26

lightweight wadding for mounting (optional)

1 skein each of stranded cotton in the following shades:

		DMC	Anchor
■	blue	336	149
■	green	895	269
■	purple	327	100
■	red	814	45
■	gold	832	907

2 skeins of stranded cotton in:

■	black	310	403

Finished size of design: 10 ¼ x 7 ½ in (26 x 19 cm)

MATERIALS

2 pieces of white Belfast linen, 32 count, each 8 x 8 in (20 x 20 cm)

tapestry needle, size 26

polyester stuffing

braid in one of the colours of the cross stitching, 18 in (45 cm) in length

1 skein each of stranded cotton in the following shades:

		DMC	Anchor
▮	blue	336	149
▮	black	310	403
▮	purple	327	100
▮	gold	832	907

Finished size of design: 2 x 2 in (5 x 5 cm)

Pincushion

The following small piece provides a further example of how you can exploit the charted designs in this book. This pincushion is worked on a fine Belfast linen and uses the fret and key patterns from the corner motif of the Horses Sampler on page 50, with the addition of two border lines. If you have already worked this sampler, you will have enough leftover threads to work this piece.

METHOD

Fold one of the pieces of linen in half lengthwise and crosswise to find the centre point. Crease lightly. Start work at this point with the centre stitch of the corner motif on the chart on page 51. Use two strands of cotton worked over two thread intersections for the cross stitch and two strands of black worked over two threads for the back stitch. When the stitching is complete, press the fabric gently from the wrong side. Place the two pieces of linen right sides together and machine stitch or back stitch by hand around three sides of the square, leaving a ¼ in (6mm) seam allowance. Trim the corners, then turn right side out. Fill the cushion with the stuffing to the desired density, then turn under the seam allowance on the open side and slip stitch to close.

Stitch the braid around all four edges of the cushion, looping it at the corners and tucking the ends into the seam allowance.

◆ **This little pincushion picks out one of the corner motifs from the Horses Sampler.**

Key and Knotwork Sampler

The traditional key patterns and knotwork of Celtic design provided the inspiration for this project, which although displayed here in picture form could also be worked as a cushion cover.

When working knotwork patterns in cross stitch, two very different effects can be achieved. A blocked effect, as that worked here, is achieved by omitting back stitched outlining. If you wish to obtain a woven effect more like the hand-drawn patterns, then use a back stitch in a shade darker than the main stitching and work continuously when the line travels over another, and break the stitching when the line passes under. Lines travel alternately over and under each other.

The effect can also be achieved by using two different colours for the lines, but beware, some knotwork is one continuous line from beginning to end: you will have to make the division into the two colours yourself. If you do choose to use the back stitch outlining, I suggest you outline as you stitch, since it can get horribly confusing to leave it all until the main stitching is finished.

The patterns for this sampler were taken from the Lindisfarne Gospels and from the Book of Kells. They can be found, however, in many other Celtic designs. Other notable sources are the Book of Durrow, the Gospel of MacDurnan and the standing stones of Pictish carvers in Scotland and in Ireland.

◆ **Intricately interlaced designs on this page from the Book of Kells are the inspiration behind this sampler.**

METHOD

This, like the other samplers, is a detailed project which will take some time to complete, so I recommend that you hem or tack the raw edges of the fabric before starting to cross stitch, to prevent them from fraying (see page 90).

Measure 3 in (7.5 cm) down from the top right corner of the fabric and 3 in (7.5 cm) in from the righthand side, and begin work at this point following the start stitch marked on the chart on page 57.

Use two strands of cotton worked over one thread intersection. If working back stitch, use two strands of cotton over one thread.

Complete each block before moving to the next via the horizontal or vertical border. Do not be tempted to work all the border first, as one miscalculated stitch will throw out the whole design. Left-handed stitchers may wish to commence with the upper left corner.

When the stitching is completed, wash if necessary and press gently from the wrong side (see page 90). For finishing and mounting instructions, see page 92.

MATERIALS

1 piece of cream Aida, 18 count, 16 x 16 in (40 x 40 cm)

tapestry needle, size 26

lightweight wadding for mounting (optional)

1 skein each of stranded cotton in the following shades:

		DMC	Anchor
■	red	350	11
■	pink	223	895
■	gold	832	907
■	dark grey	413	401
■	grey	317	400
■	dark blue	930	922
■	blue	334	977
■	rust	919	340

Finished size of design: 10 x 10 in (25 x 25 cm)

◆ Far left: The intricate weaving of geometric Celtic designs translates well into cross stitch. This sampler subtly repeats two such designs. Left: Strange creatures, key patterns and knotwork intricately fill this page from the Gospel of St John in the Lindisfarne Gospels. The corner pattern in particular has inspired the keywork in the sampler.

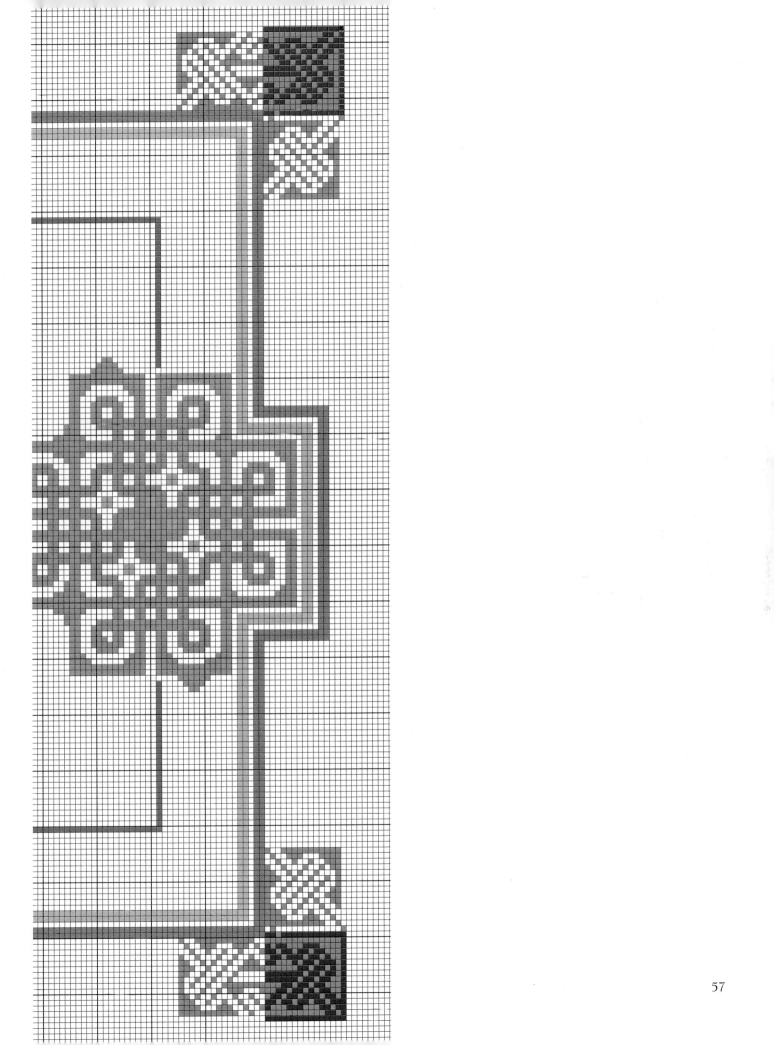

MATERIALS

2 pieces of plastic canvas, 14 count mesh, each 4 ½ x 7 in (11.5 x 18 cm)

2 pieces of lining material, same size as plastic canvas

tapestry needle, size 24

1 skein each of stranded cotton in the following shades:

		DMC	Anchor
▓	dark pink	899	40
░	light blue green	564	206

2 skeins of stranded cotton in:

▓	light brown	3773	882

3 skeins of stranded cotton in:

░	pink	818	48

Finished size of design: 4 ⅛ x 6 ¾ in (10.5 x 17 cm)

Firm Spectacles Case

Worked on plastic canvas, this key pattern is from the Lindisfarne Gospels and also appears as a corner motif on the Key and Knotwork Sampler on page 54. It is a very popular motif in Celtic art and transfers well onto many a useful cross-stitched article. It has also been used as a strip pattern on the Horses Sampler and an infill decoration on the Psalter Sampler. These two alternative uses also show the difference between forming the design purely of cross stitches and using a combination of cross and back stitch. On plastic canvas, because of its coarse mesh, it is preferable to use the pure cross stitch version. This design has been worked to a standard size. Check the size against your own spectacles and enlarge if necessary.

METHOD

Work the design on both pieces of canvas following the starting stitch on the chart on the left and leaving two holes on all sides of the canvas free.

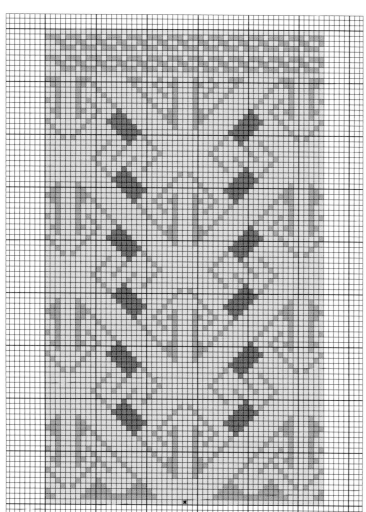

Work in cross stitch using three strands of cotton over one canvas intersection. All unshaded areas should be filled with cross stitch in pink, shade number 818 (48). When completed assemble the case as follows:

Trim the plastic canvas, leaving only one unworked row of holes all round. Place the two pieces of lining with right sides together and machine stitch or back stitch by hand together round two long and one short sides leaving a ¼ in (6 mm) seam allowance. Turn over a hem around the top opening and slipstitch in position. Lay this lining case onto the reverse side of the back sheet of worked canvas. Using one strand of the shade number 818 (48) cotton, slip stitch the base of the lining to the base of the cover. Now do the same at the top, but of course only catch one side of the lining. Next place the front sheet of the case on the other side of the lining to enclose it and slip stitch the top of the lining and canvas together.

Holding the case together oversew into the unworked holes using three strands of shade number 818 (48) all round the three sides, thus binding the back and front together. Finally oversew into the unworked holes round the opening of the case.

Easter Card

A small square design taken from a key pattern contained in the Book of Kells (see page 53) and repeated into a cross form to show the linking procedure. The design has been worked on 18 count white Aida and can be used in a card for an Easter message (as here) or a confirmation greeting. Alternatively, it could be worked on a bookmark, pot lid or bookcover, using for the latter, one of the border designs from the Psalter Sampler on page 17 to surround it. It is worked in the same shades as the pot lid on page 27.

METHOD

Fold the fabric in half lengthwise and crosswise to find the centre point. Crease lightly. Start at this point following the stitch marked on the chart on the right. Work the cross stitch using two strands of cotton over one thread intersection. Work the back stitch using one strand of cotton over one thread intersection.

When the stitching is complete, press the fabric gently from the wrong side. Place the interfacing centrally on the reverse of the work and iron in position. Trim and mount the card following the instructions on page 92.

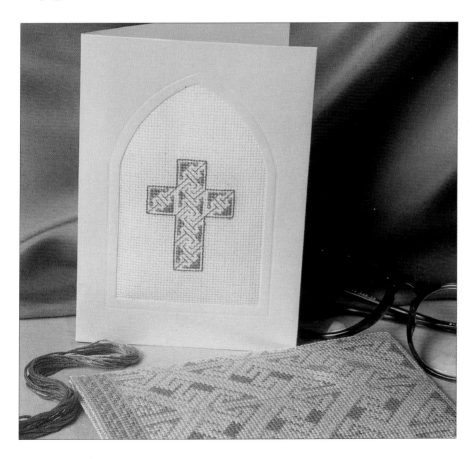

MATERIALS

1 piece of white Aida, 18 count, 5 x 7 in (12.5 x 18 cm)

1 piece of iron-on interfacing, same size as the Aida

tapestry needle, size 26

1 card blank with minimum 3 x 4 in (7.5 x 10 cm) oval cut-out (see page 93 for stockists)

1 skein each of stranded cotton in the following shades:

		DMC	Anchor
	green	733	280
	brown	680	901

Finished size of design: 1³/₄ x 2¹/₄ in (4.5 x 5.5 cm)

◆ **Two examples showing different treatments of the traditional key pattern: one an all-over design, the other a linear repeat.**

Three Designs

These three designs have all been inspired by a glorious gold and coral embellished, bronze-covered iron helmet made in the late 4th century BC. The helmet is now held at the Musée Municipale, Angoulême in France, having only been discovered in 1981 at Charente.

All the designs could be worked singly, as shown for the cross and the rosettes or as a border design, as for the petal decorations arranged like palm fronds, which are termed 'palmettes'. These palmettes are a typical 'early style' Celtic design adapted from classical sources and much favoured by the metal engravers.

◆ The cross, palmettes and rosettes featured on these four projects are all to be found in the metalworking of a Celtic bronze helmet.

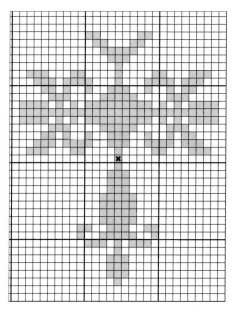

◆ The palmette designs on this 4th century gold helmet are decorated with coral studs held in place by silver rivets. Coral inlays also decorate the cheek pieces.

METHOD

Try to buy silk that has been stretched into a mount, as it is virtually unworkable in small pieces without a hoop or frame stretching it. The pre-stretched silk is also supplied with a fine needle. If you are not able to find a size 28, a size 26 can be used instead.

The silk rosette is worked in cross stitch with one strand of cotton over one thread intersection. You will need to be in a good, bright light to stitch the silk, as it is very fine work. The 16 and 18 count fabrics are worked in cross stitch with two strands over one thread intersection. Fold the fabric in half lengthwise and crosswise to find the centre point. Crease lightly. Start each project at this point following the stitch marked on the respective charts. For the band design, first decide on the length required, then fold lengthwise and crosswise to find the centre point. Work one of the motifs at this point following the start stitch on the chart on page 62. Continue to add motifs on either side leaving two spaces between the lower pink edges of the palmettes.

When the stitching is complete, press gently from the wrong side (see page 90). For the picture and notepad only, place the interfacing centrally on the reverse of the work and iron in position. Trim and mount the pieces into their frames following the manufacturer's instructions.

MATERIALS

(Picture)

1 piece of cream Aida, 16 count, 3 x 4 in (7.5 x 10 cm)

1 piece of iron-on interfacing, same size as the Aida

picture frame and mount with cut-out of 2 x 3 in (5 x 7.5 cm)

tapestry needle, size 26

1 skein each of stranded cotton in the following shades:

		DMC	Anchor
	bronze	833	907
	green	3348	264

Finished size of design: 1½ x 2 in (4 x 5 cm)

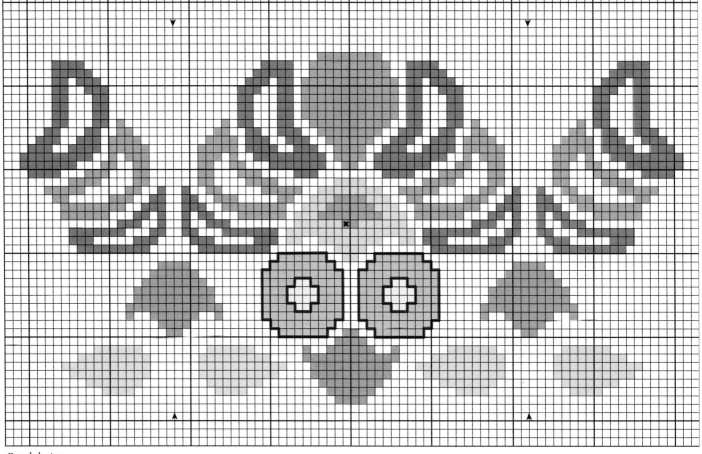

Band design

M ATERIALS

(Band)

1 piece of white Aida band, 4 in (10 cm) wide, to your required length

tapestry needle, size 26

1 skein each of stranded cotton in the following shades:

		DMC	Anchor
	deep pink	3687	68
	lilac	209	109
	blue	3755	140
	green	3348	264
	pink	3688	66
	yellow	744	301

Finished size of design (single unit): 2 ⁷⁄₈ x 2 ³⁄₄ in (7.3 x 7 cm)

(Notepad and Brooch)

1 piece of white Aida, 18 count, 3 x 3 in (7.5 x 7.5 cm), for the notepad

1 piece of white silk, 30 count, same size

as the Aida (see page 93 for stockists), for the brooch

1 piece of iron-on interfacing, same size as the Aida

tapestry needles, size 26, for the Aida and size 28 or higher, for the silk

1 notepad (see page 93 for stockists)

1 brooch mount (see page 93 for stockists)

1 skein each of stranded cotton in the following shades:

		DMC	Anchor
	pale maroon	3722	895
	gold	729	890
	grey	317	400
	pale green	471	265
	blue	809	130

Finished size of design, Aida: 1 x 1 in (2.5 x 2.5 cm)

Finished size of design, silk: ⁵⁄₈ x ⁵⁄₈ in (1.5 x 1.5 cm)

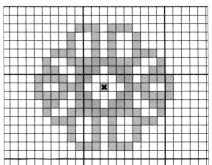

Notepad (top); Brooch (above)

Picture

Many Celtic drinking vessels and flagons of various ages have been discovered and it is one such 5th century bronze vessel which is the source of inspiration for this project. This piece was discovered in one of the rich barrow graves of the Middle Rhine at Kleinaspergle, Kr. Ludwigsburg. It is early La Tène style and shows the creative attention to innovative detail at which the Rhineland craftsmen excelled.

METHOD

Fold the fabric in half lengthwise and crosswise to find the centre point. Crease lightly. Begin work at this point following the stitch marked on the chart on page 64.

Work in cross stitch using two strands over one thread intersection. The gold metallic is worked using two strands, the other colours are worked with one strand of the colour mixed with one strand of gold metallic. When the stitching is complete, press the fabric gently from the wrong side.

Trim and mount in the picture frame, using wadding in between the embroidery and the backing board if liked.

MATERIALS

1 piece of cream Aida, 18 count, 8 x 6 in (20 x 15 cm)

picture frame, 7 x 5 in (18 x 12.5 cm), with oval cut-out

lightweight wadding for mounting (optional)

tapestry needle, size 26

1 skein each of stranded cotton in the following shades:

		DMC	Anchor
	gold	833	907
	dark gold	831	277
	green	581	280
	dark green	580	924
	gold metallic		

Finished size of design: 2 ½ x 3 ½ in (6 x 9 cm)

◆ This fine face is added as a decorative detail at the base of the handle of a 5th century bronze vessel.

◆ The curious face with flowing beard, inspired by the art of Celtic metalworkers, makes an interesting conversation-piece to hang on the wall.

Notelet Set

This notelet set and the glasses case which follows feature two lobe-shaped designs which come from different sources in different countries but are remarkably similar. The first features a design taken from an engraved bronze scabbard dated between 450 and 400 BC, which was found in a barrow at Bernkastel Wittlich in Germany. The lobe-shaped designs of this time and from this region figure strongly on many artefacts found, from jewellery to drinking vessels, and may well have been made in one or more closely linked central workshops in the Rhineland, perhaps even under Royal patronage.

MATERIALS

1 piece of cream Aida, 18 count, 5½ x 6 in (14 x 15 cm)

1 piece of iron-on interfacing, same size as the Aida

tapestry needle, size 24

1 notelet set (see page 93 for stockists)

fabric adhesive

lightweight wadding (optional)

1 skein each of stranded cotton in the following shades:

		DMC	Anchor
	bronze	834	874
	lilac	211	342
	green	772	259

Finished size of design: 2 x 2½ in (5 x 6 cm)

METHOD

Fold the fabric in half lengthwise and crosswise to find the centre point. Crease lightly. Begin work at this point following the stitch marked on the chart above.

Work in cross stitch using three strands of cotton over one thread intersection.

When the stitching is complete, press the fabric gently from the wrong side. Place the interfacing centrally on the reverse of the work and iron in position. Trim and place the fabric centrally in the mount using the same technique as for cards (see page 92) using wadding if liked.

◆ **Two fluid designs typical of middle Celtic style feature on this notelet set and spectacles case.**

◆ Two lobe-shaped designs from a bronze scabbard (top) and an open-work gold band (above).

Soft Spectacles Case

Palmettes, lobe shapes and lotus buds appear again on the source material for the second of these two lobe-shaped designs.
Of approximately the same age as the scabbard above, the openwork gold band possibly from a drinking horn from which this motif was taken, was found at Eigenbilzen in Limburg, Belgium, which was a northern extension of the Rhineland grave area.

MATERIALS

1 even-weave fabric spectacles case (see page 93 for stockists)

tapestry needle, size 26

1 skein each of stranded cotton in the following shades:

		DMC	Anchor
	pink	605	50
	green	959	186
	blue	794	175
	yellow	445	288

Finished size of design: 2 x 1 ¾ in (5 x 4.5 cm)

METHOD

Measure the flap of the spectacles case to find the centre point. Begin work at this point following the starting stitch marked on the chart above.

Work in cross stitch using two strands of cotton over one thread intersection.

Mini Picture

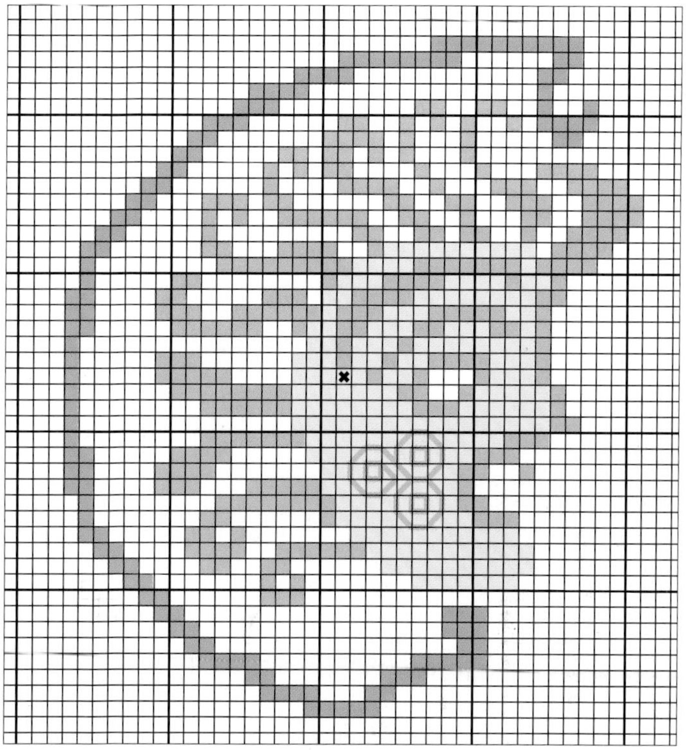

A coin of the Coriosolites from north west France, showing the head of Apollo with a very Celtic cheek-tattoo, is the source for this design, which could be mistaken for a much more modern piece. It is, in fact, from the first half of the 1st century BC. The Celts began striking their own silver and gold coins during the 4th and 3rd centuries BC. Many thousands have been excavated: some from grave sites, a find that shows the Celtic custom mirrored the common practice of other ancient cultures of providing the means for the dead to ease their passage into the afterlife. Early Celtic coins were used not so much for trading purposes but as taxes and military payments. The first designs were based on Hellenistic principles. Celtic symbols, however, soon intermingled with these, then gained precedence, so that later examples show only abstract Celtic forms.

METHOD

Fold the fabric in half lengthwise and crosswise to find the centre point. Crease lightly. Begin work at this point following the starting stitch marked on the chart above.

Use two strands of cotton worked over one thread intersection. Work the face in cross stitch and the cheek tattoo in back stitch.

When the stitching is complete, press the fabric gently from the wrong side. Place the interfacing centrally on the reverse of the work and iron in position. Trim, place the fabric centrally in the frame and assemble following the manufacturer's instructions.

MATERIALS

1 piece of white Aida, 16 count, 6 x 6 in (15 x 15 cm)

1 piece of iron-on interfacing, same size as the Aida

tapestry needle, size 26

1 round frame (see page 93 for stockists)

1 skein each of stranded cotton in the following shades:

		DMC	Anchor
	yellow	726	295
	green	581	280
	gold metallic		

Finished size of design: 2¼ x 2¾ in (5.5 x 7 cm)

◆ Celtic metalsmiths excelled at coin design. This one comes from France and is a billon coin, that is, it is made from a base metal alloyed with gold or silver.

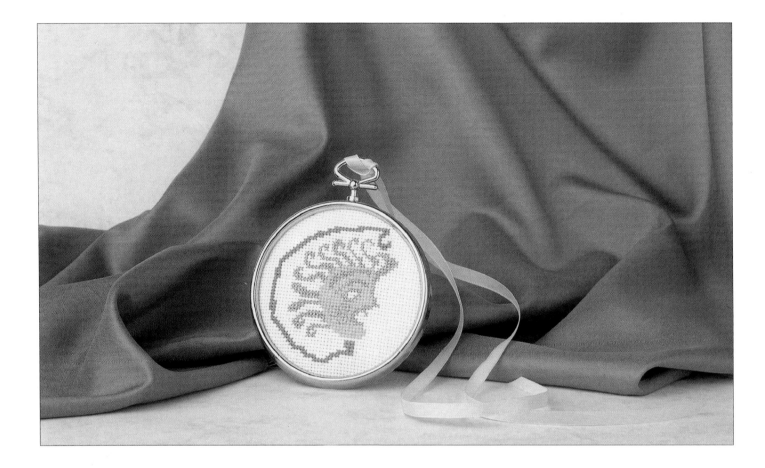

◆ A Celtic coin design translated into a
contemporary picture.

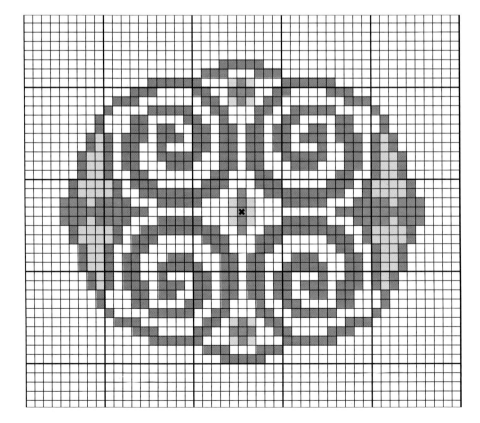

MATERIALS

(Notebook)

1 piece of cream Aida, 22 count, 4 x 4 in
(10 x 10 cm)

tapestry needle, size 26

1 indexed notebook (see page 93 for stockists)

1 skein each of stranded cotton in the
following shades:

		DMC	Anchor
	green	471	265
	bronze	832	907
	yellow	727	293

Finished size of design: 1 ⅞ x 1 ½ in
(4.75 x 4 cm)

Indexed Notebook

The spiral design work on the Battersea shield, a famous Celtic artefact, is the inspiration for this motif. This fine shield is bronze with red enamel decoration and was probably made as a show-piece or votive offering, rather than as actual battle armour. The spiral theme is to be found in all areas of decorative arts of the time from illuminated manuscript to metal scabbard and is common on pieces of jewellery.

METHOD

Fold the fabric in half lengthwise and crosswise to find the centre point. Crease lightly. Start work at this point following the stitch marked on the chart on the left.

Work in cross stitch using one strand of cotton over one thread intersection.

When the stitching is complete, press the fabric gently from the wrong side. Place the interfacing centrally on the reverse of the work and iron in position. Trim and mount the piece following the manufacturer's instructions.

◆ The Battersea shield (above) is a marvellous piece demonstrating the splendour of Celtic metal and enamel work. The spiral patterns are echoed in the notebook design (left).

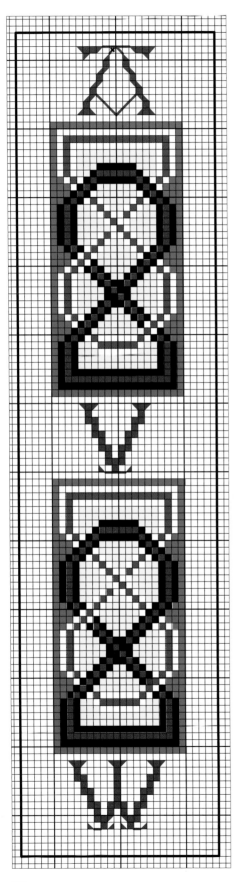

Knotwork Bookmark

Simple knotwork is featured in this design. Used in manuscripts as a single motif or in bands, I have used it here as two interlaced links to form a traditional lover's knot. This pattern is also called a 'Josephine Knot' after Napoleon Bonaparte's wife, who was a great favourite with seamen. This is a knot they commonly use. Used on a bookmark or a greetings card, it could make a rather lovely lover's gift or a token of friendship.

METHOD

The letters used to personalise this embroidery are those given on the Alphabet Sampler on pages 38-9.

   Use two strands of cotton worked over one thread intersection. Work the detail on the letters in back stitch, the rest in cross stitch.

   Fold the bookmark in half lengthwise to find the centre vertical line and mark this at the top with a pin. Check the number of threads per inch on the bookmark against the chart on the left. The bookmark counts can vary by one or two squares; if there is a discrepancy, adjust the design accordingly, so that it iscentred on the bookmark. Count down the same number of threads on the fabric as there are squares on the design chart (allowing for any discrepancy) and begin work with the starting stitch given on the chart.

   When the stitching is completed, wash if necessary and press gently from the wrong side (see page 90).

MATERIALS

1 lacy bookmark

tapestry needle, size 26

1 skein each of stranded cotton in the following shades:

		DMC	Anchor
	green	701	227
	blue	791	178
	black	310	403
	yellow	444	291
	red	321	9046

Finished size of design: 1 ¼ x 6 ¼ in (3 x 16 cm)

◆ Two personalised pieces -
a bookmark (above left) and a handy
wooden pot (left) - both make
practical, pretty gifts.

Initialled Pot Lid

This diamond-shaped design is sourced from a key pattern to be found in the Lindisfarne Gospels and has been personalised with an initial taken from the Alphabet Sampler on pages 38-9. Use the design as a card, trinket pot lid or small brooch.

MATERIALS

1 piece of white Aida, 16 count,
6 x 6 in (15 x 15 cm)

1 piece of iron-on interfacing, same size as the Aida

tapestry needle, size 26

1 wooden pot, 3 ½ in (9 cm) diameter lid (see page 93 for stockists)

1 skein each of stranded cotton in the following shades:

		DMC	Anchor
▓	pink	3687	68
▒	green	502	877

Finished size of design: 3 x 3 in (7.5 x 7.5 cm)

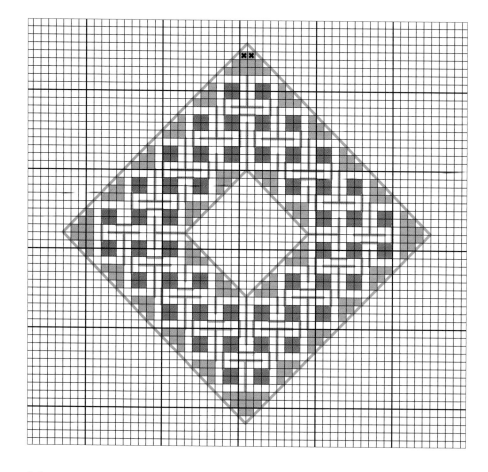

◆ **A detail from the Lindisfarne Gospels showing the complex line work at which the Celtic illuminators excelled.**

METHOD

Fold the fabric in half lengthwise to find the centre vertical line. Crease lightly. Measure 1 in (2.5 cm) down this line from the top of the fabric and place the top two green stitches on either side of this point.

Use two strands of cotton worked over one thread intersection for the cross stitch. When you have worked the main diamond, work in back stitch, using one strand of cotton over one thread of fabric, round the edge to give a clearer outline. Do the same with the inner diamond line.

When the stitching is complete, press the fabric gently from the wrong side. Place the interfacing centrally on the reverse of the work and iron in position. Trim and place the fabric centrally in the pot lid following the manufacturer's instructions.

Two Towels

Two designs to be worked on towelling. Choose towels with a flat weave band at either end. The first design is taken from a common repeat pattern of pre and Celtic art; in this case from a bronze flagon found near Salzburg, Austria. Considered to be one of the finest flagon examples of early Celtic Art, the Dürnberg flagon was excavated in 1932 and has been dated at around 450 BC. Each flagon was beaten from a single sheet of bronze with the 'comma' supports with the handle attached afterwards. Although found in Austria, the flagon's decorative work shows similarity to the Rhineland style and maybe was created by someone who had trained in the area.

This is a useful pattern to have in your collection as it is suitable for a wide variety of uses: as a frame round a message on a commemorative sampler, on towels as shown here, on cake bands, or anywhere that a border design is needed.

The hatched shell designs on a gold, glass and iron-decorated bronze helmet form the basis for the second design. The helmet was found at Amtreville-sous-les-Monts in the Eure district of France and is of 4th century BC origin. Hatched waves or shell shapes were a common fill-in device on pottery and metalwork of the Greek and Etruscan art style and were adopted by the Celts who worked them into their own designs and particularly those of the vegetal style (see page 14).

This design really does ask to be worked on towels! I have worked it in the shades of our bathroom, why not mirror the tones of your own instead?

◆ **A superb Celtic bronze flagon with fine metalwork on and around the handle.**

MATERIALS

2 towels with a flatweave band at each end
in your own choice of size and colour

waste canvas (optional)

tapestry needle, size 24

1 skein each of stranded cotton in the
following shades:

		DMC	Anchor
first design			
▨ blue	798	131
☐ yellow	307	289
▪ red	326	59
▪ lilac	553	98
second design			
▨ brown	783	307
☐ yellow	726	295

2 skeins of stranded cotton in:

| ▨ blue | 798 | 131 |

Finished size of single motif, first design:
1¼ x 1¼ in (3 x 3 cm)

Finished size of single motif, second design:
1¼ x 1⅜ in (3 x 3.5 cm)

METHOD

Work as follows for both towel designs. Fold the towel in half lengthwise
to find the central vertical line and mark with pins on the flatweave
bands, then tack. Next fold each band in half crosswise and mark with a
pin, then with tacking thread, the point at which this fold crosses the
vertical line. This gives the central point of each band. Now attach the
waste canvas
if necessary (see
page 89) and
begin stitching
the first motif at
the central point,
following the
marked stitch on
the respective
charts.

    Work in cross
stitch using three
strands of cotton
worked over one
thread intersec-
tion. Continue to
work motifs on
either side of the
first until you reach the edges. Starting in the centre will ensure that the
pattern will be evenly balanced on the band.

    If you find that the second design is too deep for the band on your
towels, work the waves or shells centrally on the band, then stitch the
border design above and below them on the fluffy parts of the towel.

    Remove the waste canvas if used. Press gently on the wrong side when
the stitching is complete.

◆ Left: Waves and shells make appropriate motifs for guest or bathtowels.

Far left: A heavily decorated bronze helmet from France. Its designs are part vegetal style and part earlier and simpler, making it a transitional piece of Celtic art.

MATERIALS

(Tea cosy)

2 pieces of white Aida, 14 count, 12 x 12 in (30 x 30 cm)

2 pieces of lining material, same size as Aida

tapestry needle, size 24

2 pieces of lightweight wadding, same size as Aida

bias binding to edge

sewing cotton to match Aida and bias binding

1 skein each of stranded cotton in the following shades:

		DMC	Anchor
	peachy brown	402	347
	deep gold yellow	783	307
	brown	356	5975
	green	501	878
	maroon	3685	69
	bright blue	824	164

Finished size of design: 11 x 7 in (28 x 18 cm)

MATERIALS

(Coaster)

1 piece of white Aida, 14 count, 4 1/2 x 4 1/2 in (11.5 x 11.5 cm)

1 piece of iron-on interfacing, same size as the Aida

tapestry needle, size 24

1 coaster set, 3 in (7.5 cm) in diameter (see page 93 for stockists)

1 skein each of stranded cotton in the following shades:

		DMC	Anchor
	green	368	214
	red	351	10
	yellow	726	295
	blue	796	133

Finished size of design: 2 x 2 1/4 in (5 x 5.5 cm)

Tea Cosy

This design combines S-shaped scrolls and whirligigs from the source material for the two towels. Suitable for a soft-line border, it can be used as shown in the photograph or split up and used separately.

METHOD

Fold one of the pieces of evenweave fabric in half lengthwise to find the centre vertical line. Crease lightly. Measure 3 in (7.5 cm) up this line from the bottom of the fabric and begin stitching one of the scrolls at this point following the starting stitch marked on the chart below.

   Work in cross stitch using three strands of cotton over one thread intersection.

   Work the design out towards each side of the fabric from this central start, stopping the stitches 1/4 in (6 mm) from the edges. Repeat with the second piece of Aida.

   Place the two pieces of fabric with right sides together. Find the centre top by folding them in half vertically again and mark this with a pin. Measure 2 in (5 cm) down the sides from each corner and mark these points with pins. Now, on the wrong side, draw a curved line from the central pin to one of the side pins. Repeat to match on the other side. Cut the fabric following this line. Now work another line of the pattern 2 in (5 cm) down from the centre top, starting with a scroll as before, so that the patterns line up at top and bottom, and finishing 1/4 in (6 mm) short of the edges. Repeat on both pieces of fabric.

   When the stitching is complete, press the two pieces of fabric gently from the wrong side, then place right sides together. Place a piece of lining on a work surface, then layer subsequent pieces centrally on top in the following order:
wadding, two pieces of embroidered Aida, second piece of wadding, second piece of lining. Machine stitch or back stitch by hand all round the curved edge through all layers, leaving a 5/8 in (1.5 cm) seam allowance. Clip the curved edge to help it to lie smoothly. Turn to the right side and bind the base of the opening with bias binding.

   Now make yourself a pot of tea, you deserve it!

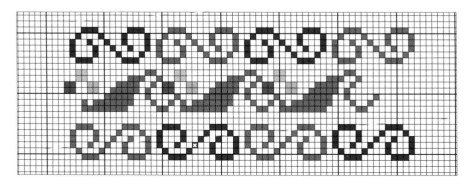

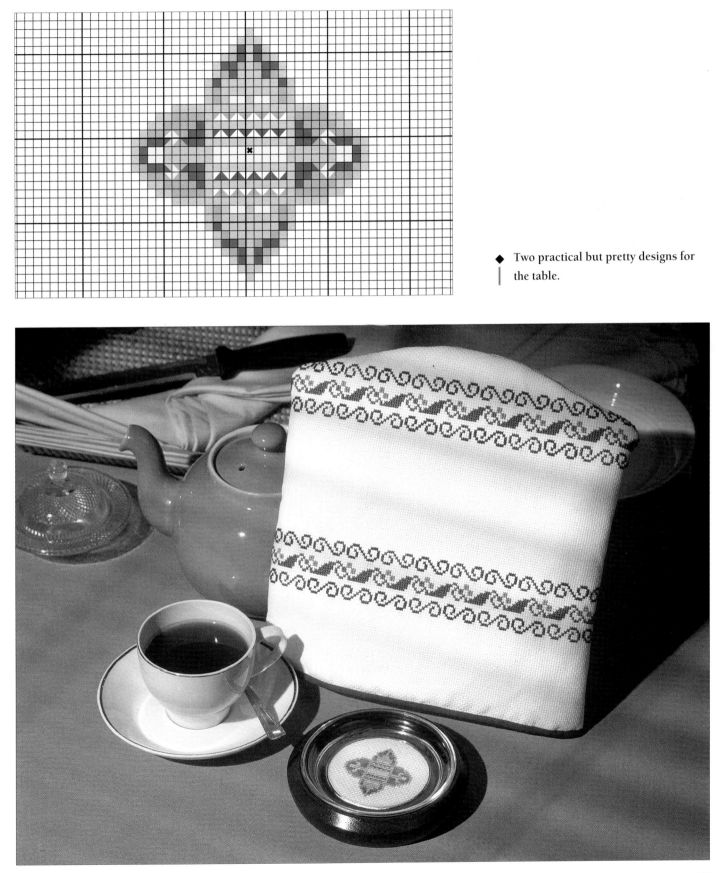

◆ Two practical but pretty designs for the table.

Coasters

An enamelled trapping from the Polden Hills, Somerset find is the design source for these coasters. Dating from the 1st century AD and found during ploughing in 1803 the 'Polden Hills Hoard' was a substantial find of horse-fittings and shield bosses, possibly an ancient scrap merchant's stock! Many of the pieces are enamelled with or have inlays of coloured glass, beautifully hued in green, red, yellow and blue which I have tried to reflect in this design.

Shown here as a single motif, this design could be also be used for a repeat border.

METHOD

Fold the fabric in half lengthwise and crosswise to find the centre point. Crease lightly. Start work at this point following the stitch marked on the chart on page 77.

Work in cross stitch using three strands of cotton over one thread intersection.

When the stitching is complete, press the fabric gently from the wrong side. Place the interfacing centrally on the reverse of the work and iron in position. Trim and place the fabric centrally in the mount following the manufacturer's instructions.

◆ This kind of harness decoration was probably used to conceal the junction of two straps. The trappings have two loops at the back to anchor the harness and are made of bronze with rich and colourful enamelling.

Chart-only samplers

This final section of the book features three very different aspects of Celtic design: illuminated manuscript, metalwork and stone carving. The artefacts are shown in full page photographs alongside each of which is a cross stitch chart demonstrating a possible interpretation of the original. These pieces can be stitched by following the chart exactly and will make stunning samplers in their own right. Alternatively, they can be adapted to your own requirements or split up and used as a motif library. Details on how to estimate the size of fabric required are given on page 92.

PAGES 80 TO 82
ILLUMINATED CANON PAGE SAMPLER

As discussed on page 36, a canon page in an illuminated manuscript lists cross references between the four Gospels of the New Testament. This page is from the Harley Gospels dated around 800 AD. The chart has simplified the structure and the text areas have been left blank for you to add your own personal details. You could use them to record family birthdays or you could omit the horizontal lines and add two special names vertically in between the columns.

PAGES 83 TO 85
SUTTON HOO CLASP SAMPLER

The photograph shows an intricately crafted shoulder clasp which was part of the amazing treasures discovered at the ship-burial site at Sutton Hoo, England, in 1939. This beautiful piece is made of gold inlaid with garnets and millefiori glass. It is probably sixth century. The design of the step-sided cells is echoed in the carpet pages of the Lindisfarne Gospels (see, for example, page 55) and it is thought that the illuminators of the Gospels may well have been inspired by the clasp. The colour scheme of the chart assumes you will be stitching onto a white or cream fabric. However, you could choose a red fabric and use a complementary set of yellow, gold and orange threads instead.

PAGES 86 TO 88
STONE CROSS SAMPLER

Several Celtic crosses are still standing. This one is a High Cross which can be seen in the Kidalton churchyard on Islay in Scotland. It has relief carving and the typical stone ring joining the arms to the shaft of the cross. The chart recreates the shape, then fills in the segments of the cross with spiral and keywork patterns taken from other designs in the book. You can, of course, work your own selection of patterns within the outlines.

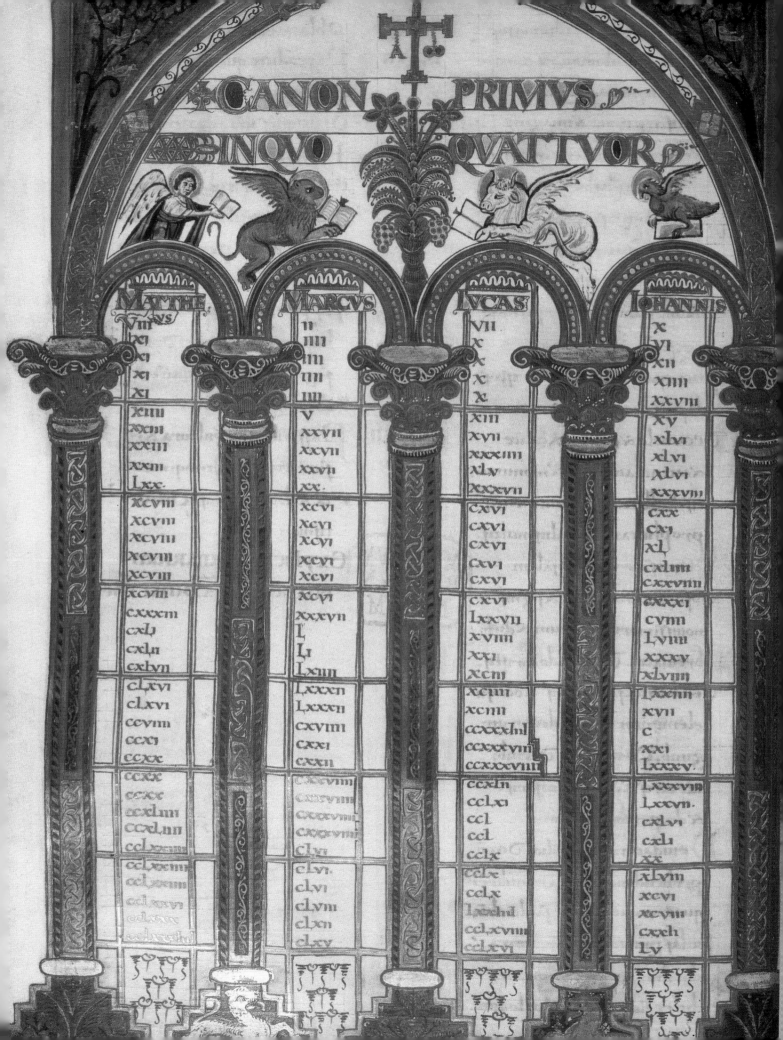

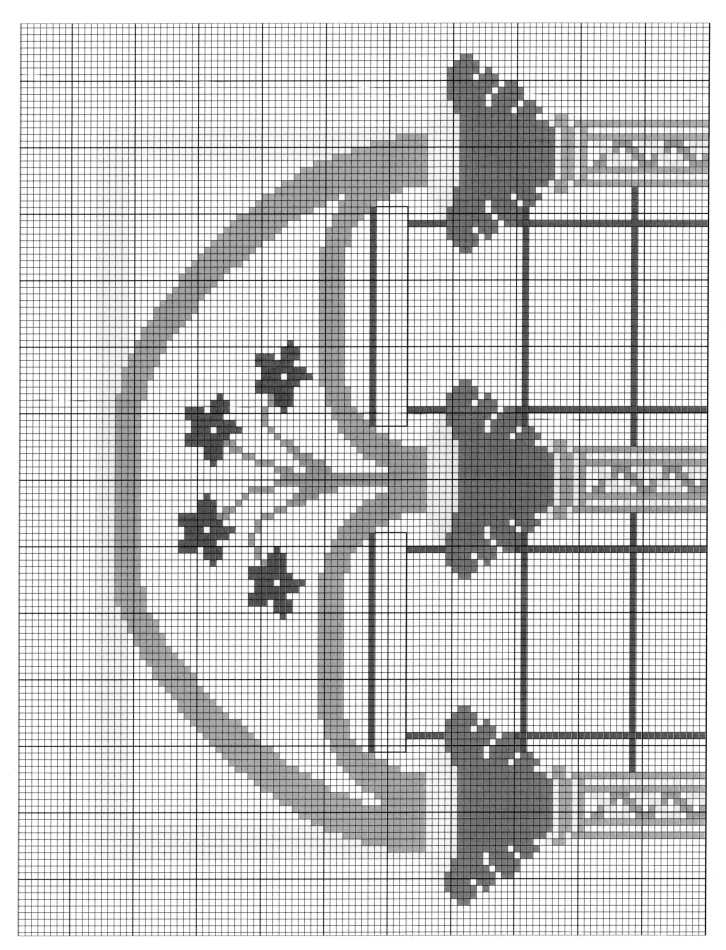

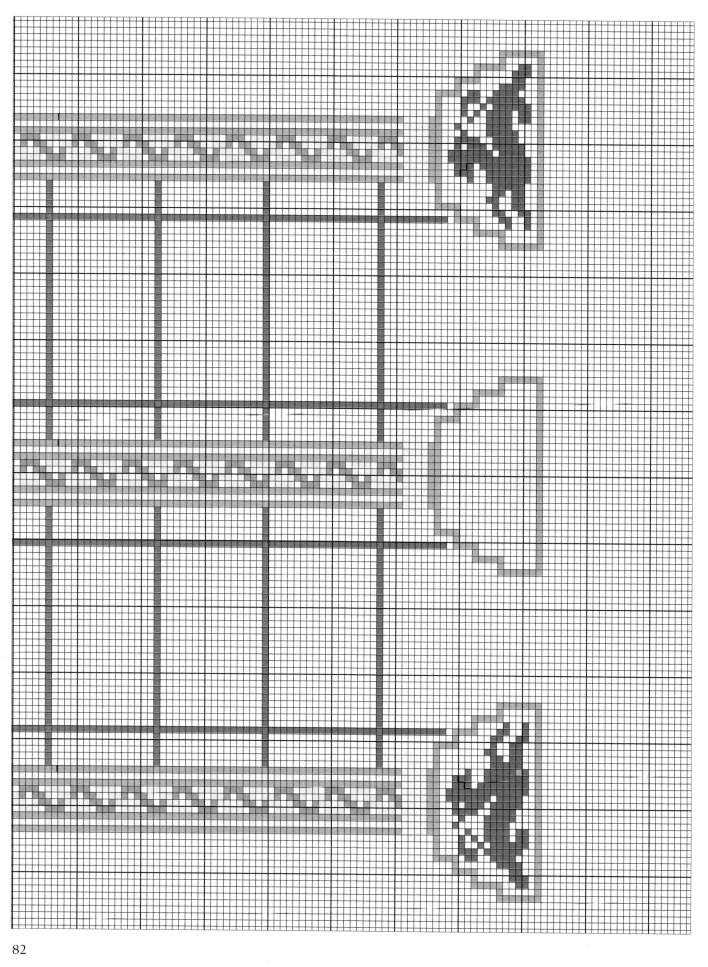

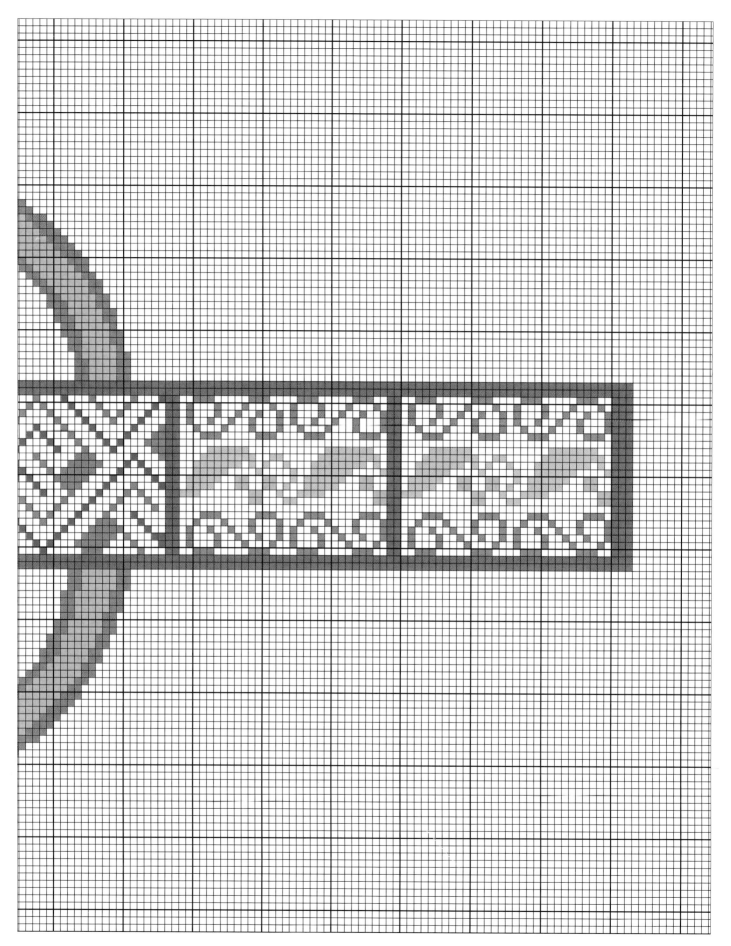

Practical Details

FABRICS

Cross stitch is mostly worked on evenweave fabrics - those which have a well-defined, equal warp (vertical) and weft (horizontal) thread, woven in such a way that there are the same number of warp as of weft threads in any square of fabric. Evenweave fabric comes in a variety of types and sizes, which are graded according to the number of threads or holes per inch with the highest number denoting the finest weave and consequently producing the finest stitch. This grading of fabric is referred to as the 'count' of the fabric, so that 18 count fabric will have 18 holes and threads to the inch (2.5 centimetres). Grades range from 10 count through to 26. If a novice, I suggest you start with projects on a lower count (14, for example) and when you are conversant with the basic skill move to the finer or higher counts.

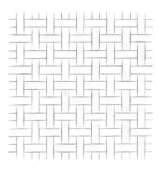

Aida is a widely available type of evenweave fabric and many of the projects in this book are worked on it in various counts. It is woven with groups of warp and weft threads bulked together and woven as one unit, which leaves clearly defined holes between and makes it easy to see where to place the stitches.

Hardanger, a type of evenweave in which pairs of threads are woven together, is also available and the same principles apply.

Lugana is another type of evenweave. A 25 count is available in a variety of shades and is a lovely fabric for bellpulls and wall hangings, as it is softer than Aida but weightier, so that it hangs well. It also has the advantage that, like linens, it can be worked over one or two threads.

Also featured in this book are products made from 'Sal-Em' fabric, an American-produced fabric, cut to the shape of napkins or traycloths with frayed edges and a pre-stitched line around the edges to prevent further fraying. It can be used either for fine stitches worked over one thread to form 26 count or over two threads to form 13 count. If unavailable, a 26 count linen could be used. You could, then, either hem or fray the edges yourself.

Linen is also suitable. This is a plain-weave, i.e. a fabric in which a single weft is woven alternately over and under a single warp, but is still suitable for cross-stitch work as the weaving of the warp and weft threads is equally spaced throughout the fabric.

Special silk fabric is also used, this has a very high count and needs to be stretched into a frame, to make it manageable for stitching. It is available in pre-stretched form (see page 93) and is supplied with a fine needle. Make sure you are working in a good, bright light when stitching silk, as it is very fine work.

All the fabrics come in a variety of shades and colours. I have used mostly cream and white in this series, but do try experimenting with other shades. Maybe your specialist needlecraft store has a few remnant pieces you could try at not too high a cost for experimentation.

Waste canvas

Other fabrics can be used if your eye and patience are good, but do not attempt to use these until you have mastered the craft.

Waste canvas, available from specialist stores can help with the stitching of non-defined fabric, that is fabric which does not have an obvious grid of threads to work over, such as towelling or velvet. Waste canvas provides a temporary grid, which can be removed after it has been stitched over.

Pin or tack a piece of waste canvas 1 in (2.5 cm) larger all round than the design to be stitched onto the fabric you wish to embroider. Work your stitches over it but be careful not to pull up the stitches too tightly. Once the stitching is

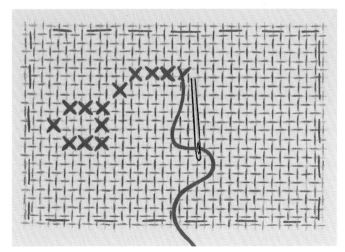

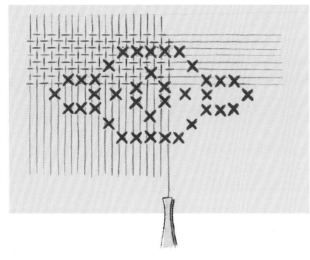

completed, draw out the threads of the waste canvas one by one with tweezers. They should release quite easily as long as your tension has not been too severe!

Care of fabric

All the evenweaves and linen launder beautifully and the stranded cottons used throughout the books are colourfast. If you are in any doubt about whether your threads are colourfast, do a test wash using a little of all the colours on a small piece first. When you have completed your project, if you feel it has become slightly grubby from handling, just wash gently in warm, soapy water, then rinse, to revitalise it. You will also be able to re-stiffen the evenweave Aida by doing this, which will make it easier to mount, as it does tend to soften while being worked. Roll up the embroidery in a dry towel to take out excess moisture, then leave the work on a flat surface to dry naturally. When dry, gently press the embroidery from the wrong side on a dry towel base with a medium-hot steam iron. The fabric can also be given a gentle press in this way during the stitching of a large project, if you feel it has become too limp.

THREADS

Every shade imaginable can be purchased! Half the fun is deciding which to use. Metallic threads are also popular and can add quite a sparkle to your work but the mainstay thread for cross stitch is stranded cotton. It is so-called because each thread is made up of six strands, which are separated to work with, the number of strands altering dependent on the count of the fabric.

As a rough guide on 10 to 14 count use three strands (unless the design is so dense you prefer to use two strands on 14); on 16 to 22 use two strands and on higher counts, one strand.

Other threads, such as crochet cotton, Danish flower threads, coton à broder and stranded silk are also suitable for cross stitch, though the thicker single strand threads should only be used on low counts of fabric.

Use of threads

As suggested, use different numbers of strands for different counts of fabric but universally do not thread your needle with more than a 14 in (35 cm) length at any time. A longer thread will eventually fray in the needle as it is drawn repeatedly through the fabric and leave a feathery thread on the stitching; it may, indeed, even fray out and break.

NEEDLES

Always use blunt-ended tapestry needles. The general rule regarding size is that the eye of the needle should be able to pass through the fabric without distorting the weave and leaving a larger hole. Size 24 is perfect for counts up to 14 and size 26 is fine for other higher counts; on silk use an even finer needle - size 28 or higher - as these are often up to 48 count!

FRAMES

Hoop frames are often used to prevent distortion of the fabric caused by an over-tight tension. Try a small one if you wish, your needlecraft shop will advise you and let you handle the various sizes to see which is comfortable for you. Personally, I only use one when working with floppy fabrics to help keep my tension even. I find generally I like to be able to manoeuvre the fabric in my hands without the constraint of the hoop, the natural stiffness of some fabrics being enough to keep tension balanced. So, whether or not to use a frame is very much your choice.

SETTING TO WORK

Before starting fix a short piece of each thread to a strip of card and number it. This will help you identify the shade, invaluable if you find yourself working in a poor light (which should be avoided) or artificial light when tones, particularly of blues, greens and pinks can subtly alter.

With larger projects it is best (time consuming, I know) to protect the edges of the fabric to prevent fraying, which linen, in particular, is prone to do. To do this, either turn under a small hem all round and tack down or bind the edges with masking tape. This is generally unnecessary with small projects.

The starting point on a stitching chart is generally indicated, as is the case for all the projects in these books. For small designs this is usually in the centre, so that it is helpful to be able to find the centre of your fabric quickly. To do this fold the fabric in half lengthwise and crosswise and crease lightly. For larger projects you may find it useful to tack through the centre vertical and horizontal lines created by folding the fabric, so that these provide permanent reference points when stitching the design. On smaller projects just the creased cross should be enough to get you started. Some patterns give the start stitch in one corner or in the middle of one edge of the pattern, so you will not need to do the above tacking or creasing, just follow the instructions as to the start point.

Thread your needle with the directed number of strands. Do not knot the end as this creates lumps which make an uneven surface on the embroidery and knots can unravel. To commence the first stitch, pull the thread through from the reverse side leaving a tail of about 2 inches (5 cm).

◆ **Single cross stitch**

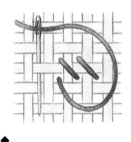

◆

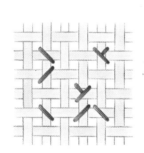

Hold this tail under the fabric as you work the next stitch. After a few stitches you can either darn the tail in at the back or catch it under with the subsequent stitches. Fasten off by drawing the thread, on the reverse side, through the back of some stitches.

◆ **Half cross stitch**

All the projects in this book use simple cross stitch for most of the design, half cross stitch for some of the shaping and back stitch for outlining. Use the simple half cross stitch for shaping on the edge of a motif and the three quarters version when required in the middle of a design.

If you are a novice, follow the diagrams on a spare piece of fabric to practise.

It is important that the top half of the stitches should all slant in the same direction, otherwise the finished work will look uneven.

All the patterns are worked from colour charts. One square on the chart represents one stitch worked over one or two thread inter-sections on the fabric as directed in the individual instructions. Half squares on the chart denote half cross

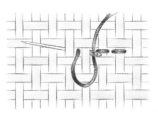

◆ **Backstitch**

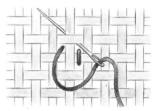

◆ **Angled backstitch**

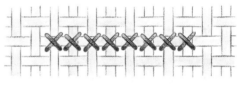

◆ **Over one thread intersection**

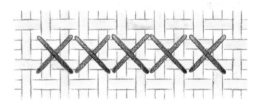

◆ **Over two thread intersections**

stitches, the direction of the diagonal indicating the direction of the stitch. If stitches of one shade are scattered close by each other but not immediately abutting each other, it is acceptable to thread the strands through the backs of some of the other stitches to the next point of stitching, but do this only where there is close proximity of stitch, otherwise the overall tension will become distorted.

Using more than one needle

It is useful, when working a design where groups of stitches in the same shade are close to each other, to use more than one needle. When you have stitched the first group, take the needle through to the reverse of the fabric and secure it loosely in a position where it will not interfere with the next stitches you will work. Using the second needle, work the second shade and fasten the needle at the back of the work, as before. Now remove the first needle and thread it through the back of the stitches just worked, so that it is in the right position to work the second group of stitches in the first shade. This can only be done where groups of stitches in the same shade are separated by just three or four squares. If you carry thread over a larger distance, you may produce an uneven tension and on a low count of fabric the lines of thread may show through to the front.

It is also helpful to have several needles threaded with different shades at the start of a complicated project. This saves time once you are stitching.

Estimating fabric size

The finished size of the stitching area is given with each project, so that if you wish to adapt the design you can work out how the dimensions will change.

If you wish to work one of the projects in this book on a different count of fabric from that recommended, you will need to calculate how much fabric to allow, which is very simple. Count the number of squares on the design chart a) down one vertical edge and b) across one horizontal edge. Divide each of these figures by the count of the fabric you wish to use, e.g. by 14 or 16. This will give you the finished design size in inches. Multiply by 2.54 if you wish to have the size in centimetres.

If the work is to be mounted in a frame, add 6 in (15 cm) to each dimension for the fabric size. This allows a good 3 in (7.5 cm) for the framer to use and a 1 in (2.5 cm) hem allowance (to prevent fraying while working).

For fabric size on smaller projects, add 3 in (7.5 cm) to the dimensions of the design, and to fit a particular mount, measure its width and depth, then add on 3 in (7.5 cm).

Letter spacing

This is best worked out on graph paper first, to give a good visual image of how the letters will look. Map out the letters in each horizontal row in pencil on the graph paper, leaving one stitch square between each letter and three between each word. Note that letters which have sloping sides, such as A, W, V, may look better more closely grouped, i.e. without the unstitched square in between.

Now count up the number of horizontal squares in the row and divide by two to find the central point. Where the letters are to be placed centrally on the design, this point will correspond to the centre vertical line of the design. Begin stitching at this point.

For designs where the text is positioned off-centre, refer to the appropriate chart for the starting point. Do map out the letters on graph paper first, though, as you may need to adjust the placing slightly.

FINISHING OFF AND MOUNTING

Tidy your work as you stitch, fastening each thread off by darning it into the back other stitches. Snip off any loose ends.

If the piece needs to be cleaned or freshened up, follow the instructions for washing and pressing given above.

Mounting into card-based mounts, e.g. calendars, greeting cards

Trim the finished piece of work to a slightly smaller size than the mount. Touch fabric adhesive to the edges of the mount and with the design uppermost on a flat surface, place the mount, centrally or as directed, onto the design. At this stage you can pad the design with a little wadding to bring it forward in the mount and soften the edges of the cut-out area. To do this, cut a piece of lightweight wadding just a little larger than the aperture of the mount, touch with glue and fix to the reverse of the embroidered piece. Next glue around the edges of the back of the card or mount backing board and attach it to the back of the embroidery, enclosing the design. Take your time, I have seen too many examples of beautiful stitchwork ruined by bad mounting.

Pots and jars

Back your work with iron-on interfacing before placing in the mount. This has a dual purpose a) it will help prevent fraying and b) it will enable the design to sit more firmly in the mount and not crumple. Iron the interfacing on before you trim the fabric to size. Follow the manufacturers' instructions to assemble the mounts, which are usually simply a matter of trimming the embroidery to fit and placing it in the jar or pot with the backing material in a particular sequence.

Pictures

It is well worth paying for professional mounting. All the effort you have put into the stitching deserves the best!

I like to stretch my work over lightweight wadding as I think it gives a good relief, softening the lines and pushing the stitching forward. A professional framer will lace the work with the wadding over the backing board for you.

A FINAL WORD

Do keep your work in a bag in between stitching: the fabric does tend to pick up dust. But most importantly, after all the rules of 'do's and don'ts', enjoy your craft, be experimental and have fun with creating and stitching the heirlooms of the future!

ACKNOWLEDGEMENTS
The Author and Publishers would like
to thank the following people for their
help in the production of this book:

For supplying props for photography:
Past Times, Witney, Oxon,
OX8 6BH, UK

Rhiannon, The Welsh Gold Centre,
Tregaron, Dyfed SY25 6JL, Wales

For supplying materials for the projects:
DMC Creative World, Pullman Road,
Wigston, Leicestershire,
LE18 2DY, UK

Framecraft Miniatures Ltd,
372-376 Summer Lane, Hockley,
Birmingham, B19 3QA, UK
(with stockists worldwide)

Impress, Slough Farm, Westhall,
Halesworth, Suffolk IP19 8RN, UK

Kernowcraft Woodturning,
The Courtyard Shopping Mews, 9 High
Street, St Ives, Cornwall, TR26 1RS, UK

For help with the stitching:
Sally Harvey; Sally Mason; Barbara
Matthews

For help with research:
Julie Davies at Oriel Gallery, The Friary,
Cardiff, Wales

The British Museum,
London WC1N 3AF, UK

STOCKISTS
Brooch; coasters; clock; desk pen set;
fabric spectacles case; lacy bookmark;
pre-stretched silk; round frame;

Sal-Em products; wooden pot:
Framecraft Miniatures Ltd

Greetings cards; indexed notebook;
notelet set; notepad: Impress

Little wooden pot: Kernowcraft

KITS
All the stitched projects within this book
may be purchased in kit form
(excluding charts) from:
Stitchkits, 8 Danescourt Road,
Tettenhall, Wolverhampton,
WV6 9BG, UK

PHOTOGRAPH CREDITS
p.10 Museum of Archaeology and
Anthropology, University of Cambridge;
p.12, p.49 Grammar of Ornament,
Studio Editions, 1986; p.13 Derek
Laird/Still Moving Pic Co, p.86 Paul
Tomkins/S T B Still Moving; p.15 and
p.35, p.19, p.40, p.74 C M Dixon;
p.16, p.26, p.29, p.34, p.41, p.46,
p.53 The Board of Trinity College,
Dublin; p.32 E T Archive/British
Library, p.69 E T Archive/British
Museum, p.80 E T Archive/British
Museum; p.34, p.55 British Library;
p.61 Gamma/Patrimoine 2001; p.63
Württembergisches Landesmuseum,
Stuttgart; p.67 Bibliothèque Nationale;
p.73 Salzburger Museum Carolino
Augusteum; p.78 Horae Ferales, Lovell
Reeve & Co, 1863; p.83 Michael
Holford